# THE
# WESTMINSTER
# HISTORICAL DATABASE

## VOTERS,
## SOCIAL STRUCTURE
## AND ELECTORAL BEHAVIOUR

# THE WESTMINSTER HISTORICAL DATABASE

## VOTERS, SOCIAL STRUCTURE AND ELECTORAL BEHAVIOUR

**Charles Harvey**
**Edmund M. Green**
**and Penelope J. Corfield**

Published by
Bristol Academic Press
7 Grange Park
Westbury-on-Trym
Bristol
BS9 4BU

British Library Cataloguing-in-Publication Data.
A catalogue record for this book is
available from the British Library.

ISBN
0 9513762 5 X (book)
0 9513762 6 8 (CD-ROM)

Typeset by Bristol Academic Press and
Printed in Great Britain by
Antony Rowe Ltd.
Chippenham
England
SN14 6QA

# Contents

**Tables**

**Figures**

**Illustrations**

**Conventions**

| | Place of publication is London unless otherwise stated. |
|---|---|
| BL | British Library, London. |
| BM | British Museum, London. |
| *B.P.P.* | *British Parliamentary Papers.* |
| George | F.G. Stephens and M.D. George (eds), *Catalogue of political and personal satires preserved in the Department of Prints and drawings in the British Museum* (11 vols, 1870-1954). |
| Green, 'Thesis' | E.M. Green, 'Social structure and political allegiance in Westminster, 1774-1820', (unpub. Ph.D. thesis, University of London,1992). |
| Guildhall | Guildhall Library, London. |
| LMA | London Metropolitan Archives (formerly Greater London Record Office), London. |
| *O.E.D.* | *The Oxford English Dictionary* (20 vols, Oxford, 1989). |
| PRO | Public Record Office, London. |
| WAC | City of Westminster Archives Centre (formerly Westminster City Library, Department of Archives and Local History), London. |

# Preface

This book provides a detailed guide to the Westminster Historical Database. Version 1 of the Database has been released by the authors into the public domain as a resource for historians interested in occupations, social structure and political behaviour in eighteenth- and early nineteenth century England. It is available on a CD-ROM published by Bristol Academic Press as a companion to this book.

The Database is the product of many years of hard labour and careful scholarship. It consists of 23 two-way tables in standard relational format. Of these, 12 are electronic editions of the surviving Westminster Poll Books for the years between 1749 and 1820, enhanced through the addition of supplementary fields for name and occupational codes. A further 9 tables are versions of selected Westminster Parish Rate Books which complement the Poll Book tables and which, through record linkage, enable a much fuller representation to be made of Westminster's voters, their social standing and political preferences. The remaining two Database tables contain coding schema for names and occupations respectively.

The strength of the Westminster Historical Database, in version 1 at least, lies not so much in its size as in its richness. The core Poll and Rate tables contain 143,840 records, and the two code book tables hold an additional 25,704 records. Whilst in absolute terms this is a large number of records, when compared with contemporary corporate or government data banks it is not the size of the Database which impresses. What does impress, however, is the fact that the data relate to *named* individuals, their social characteristics and their voting behaviour. Few databases in the world contain such detailed information on individual people and their actions at key moments in history.

It is useful to think of the Westminster Historical Database as being akin to a scholarly edition. Such editions typically consist of two parts: a preferred version of a text or set of texts, and a critical or analytical scholarly apparatus. Judicious use of the scholarly apparatus enables the editor(s) of the text(s) to explain and justify a long stream of often sophisticated editorial judgements and to present illuminating contextual material. In modern parlance, a good edition has a large amount of *value added* through the scholarly apparatus.

The Westminster Historical Database may be likened to a carefully edited set of texts and this book to its accompanying scholarly apparatus. The intention of the authors is to add value to the Database in five principal ways. First, the book documents the primary sources used to compile the Database and justifies the selection of material. Secondly, numerous editorial decisions are recorded and explained, thereby enabling the user to make technical modifications and adjustments in the full light of prior decisions. Thirdly, the structure of the Database is detailed for ease of use and the avoidance of error. Fourthly, the book enumerates and defines the numerous codes contained in Poll Book and Rate Book tables. Without these codes, it would be problematic to extract meaningful information from the Database. Finally, three key topics in historical computing are discussed at some length: the classification of occupations, information retrieval, and the devising of effective record linkage strategies and procedures. The aim is to equip users of the Database with the technical and conceptual knowledge needed to get the most out of it and to benefit from original research conducted by the authors.

Each of the authors has had a long standing interest in historical sources and methods. The potential for using computers to implement new and ambitious research strategies and to create easily transportable research resources gave rise to the Westminster Historical Database. Many others have seen the same promise and have risen to the particular challenges of database-centred research. Yet it remains true that most historical databases, whether or not they have been deposited in a data archive, suffer from poor documentation and a lack of systematic editing: they do not have the scholarly apparatus comparable to those of the best printed editions. We have endeavoured therefore not to fall into the trap of allowing the short term need to publish research results to detract from the fundamental tasks of ensuring that our work is systematic, precisely documented and replicable. These, we believe, are the basic tenets to which all historical databases should be subject before release to the general community of historians.

The above remarks should not be taken to mean that the authors believe their work to be perfect in every respect. Any such claim would be both pompous and unsustainable. It would have been possible, for example, with additional time, effort and resources to have revised the occupational classification and to have integrated the scholarly apparatus presented here in book form with the Database itself. Additional resources equally would have allowed the Database to be extended and deepened in several valuable ways. However, the authors would ask users of the Database to respect the integrity of what has been accomplished to date. Version 1 of the Westminster Historical Database has the capacity for further development. The authors do not wish this to be entered into lightly or without due consideration. We are ready to collaborate with others subject to the condition that the process of upgrading the Database is managed to agreed standards. We would expect future versions to appear together with new, relevant research and definitive copies to be deposited with the History Data Service of the Economic and Social Research Council (ESRC) Data Archive at the University of Essex (UK).

The Westminster Historical Database could not have been created and published without the support of the Economic and Social Research Council. The authors wish to record their gratitude to the ESRC for its financial support, and for its encouragement of interdisciplinary investigation into both substantive and methodological issues. This has facilitated the project *Choice and change in a mass electorate: the City of Westminster, 1749-1820* (award no. R000236309).

We are grateful also to those individuals who have aided our work: to Sheila Anderson for archiving the data; to Meg Davies for the index; to Catherine Harbor for technical advice and assistance especially on information retrieval and record linkage; to Philip Hartland for help in designing and developing the Database; to Justin Jacyno for the map; to Serena Kelly for assistance with occupational coding; to Jon Press for help with information retrieval and the bibliography; to Kevin Schürer for guidance on best practice in archiving data; to Philip Taylor for help with the front cover; and to Matthew Woollard for the Soundex codes and much patient help.

Finally we are grateful to those institutions which have facilitated our work: the Department of History and the School of Management

at Royal Holloway, University of London; the Institute of Historical
Research; the London Metropolitan Archives; the British Museum;
and the City of Westminster Archives Centre.

Charles Harvey
Edmund M. Green
Penelope J. Corfield
March 1998

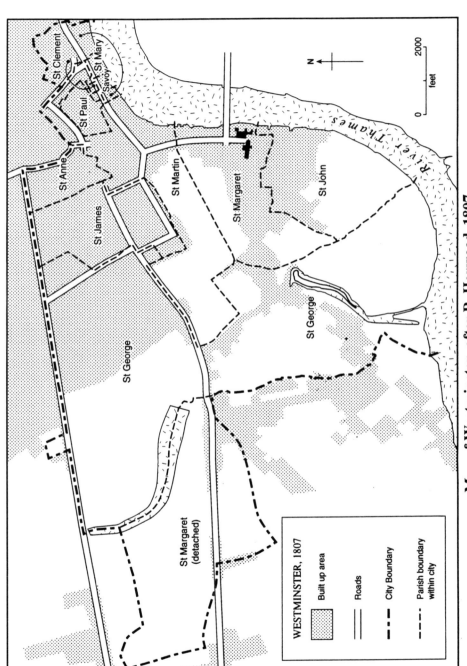

Map of Westminster, after R. Horwood, 1807

St Clement

St Mary
Savoy

St Paul

St Anne

St James

St Martin

St Margaret

St John

St George

St George

St George

St Margaret
(detached)

River Thames

N

0          2000
feet

WESTMINSTER, 1807

Built up area

Roads

City Boundary

Parish boundary
within city

# 1

# Introduction

'Earth has not anything to show more fair', wrote William Wordsworth in 1802, marvelling at the view from Westminster Bridge of
the great metropolis. It was a gracious tribute from the man from
Cockermouth, who was in general no lover of the urban anthill. Of
course, the sonnet famously referred to London at dawn, when the
inhabitants were sound asleep, their collective bustle temporarily
abated. Yet Wordsworth's poem acknowledged the latent power of
this mass of people, the 'mighty heart' of England. And in *The
Prelude* (1805 version) he showed that he had observed the waking
life of the city streets as well:

> ...strangers of all ages, the quick dance
> Of colours, lights and forms, the Babel din,
> The endless stream of men and moving things
> ... The comers and the goers face to face –
> Face after face ...'.[1]

Historians, however, follow but slowly in the footsteps of fleet-
ing poets. Successive generations of scholars have done much to
clarify aspects of life in London.[2] At the same time, however, there
remain great gaps in historical knowledge that tend to be filled, if
they are filled at all, by untested assumptions. Surprisingly little is
known in detail about the lives of ordinary Londoners at the time
when Wordsworth was writing. Much of the evidence that remains
is scrappy or impressionistic or partial. Systematic analysis thus
becomes problematic. And, above all, it is hard to find evidence
that stretches across the social spectrum, so that the historian can
investigate simultaneously the activities of the great aristocrat and
Wordsworth's humble 'scavenger that begs with hat in hand'.

With this book, of course, we cannot claim to resolve all the
evidential problems relating to the history of metropolitan London
and (by 1801) its 900,000 inhabitants. There are always more

questions than answers, more debates than data. Rather, this survey provides a guide to one remarkable set of consistent, abundant and wide-ranging source of information that has survived; and indicates how the material can be analysed systematically.

The historian standing, with Wordsworth, on Westminster Bridge in 1802 would be looking closely at the City of Westminster, the western pole of Britain's sprawling metropolis. There lived dukes, ministers of state, bishops, financiers, businessmen and lawyers – alongside the unglamorous labourers, scavengers,[3] night-soilmen and grave-diggers. The number of potential human encounters within the Westminster population of approximately 153,000 residents in 1801 was enormous. And the crowds of bustling city residents were continually swelled by country visitors, like Wordsworth who acknowledged himself as a 'transient visitant' on his first visit there in 1788. Much of the detail of the lives and life styles of this huge population is irrecoverable by historians.

Yet there were significant moments when many Westminster citizens acted together with common purpose. These were occasions when they went to cast their votes during the great contested elections in the years between 1749 and 1820. Certainly, there was more to life than voting. And, equally certainly, not all local residents were passionate political partisans. The Westminster elections were, however, great civic moments. Before the 1832 Reform Act, the constituency was by far the largest in the country that went regularly to the polls. As such, it saw a series of especially memorable confrontations, especially those between Charles James Fox, the hero of the Whigs, and his conservative opponents. Westminster was taken to be the battleground for popular opinion. The contests were therefore undertaken in a highly charged atmosphere, with excited canvassing, high turnouts, lively street encounters, heated arguments, many amusing satirical prints, and much political passion.

Thence comes the interest for the historian. Large numbers of male voters publicly identified themselves by name, parish (or place) of residence, and occupation; and, if unchallenged, cast their votes. Given the size of the electorate,[4] this provides a substantial body of important information about the work, residence and political affiliation of thousands of Westminster citizens. Wordsworth himself, despite lodging in London on more than one occasion, did not attend at the polls. But many others did so, including in 1790 the poet and artist William Blake, who confidently plumped with a single vote for Fox. All this provides invaluable information about both the famous and the obscure. Furthermore, the data can be cross-matched with other sources to yield further insights. In particular, as Westminster had a rate-paying franchise,[5] crucial information about the financial status of voters can be ascertained through record linkage.[6] In other words, the public life (voting behaviour) and personal identity (residence, occupation, civic status) of all voters were simultaneously on show.

That confers upon the evidence a strong testament of reliability, especially since in case of doubt a voter could be challenged. Despite the surrounding hubbub, the procedures were taken with great seriousness. Parish officials attended with documentary evidence to check the voters' *bona fides* [see illustration on front cover]. Charles James Fox himself reported on the procedure to Parliament in 1784:[7]

> The parish books were constantly at the hustings, and each voter's name, profession, and description, collated with the books ... When the names of voters could not always be found in the parish books ... a gentleman in the interest of each side frequently went to the very street in which the voter said he lived; that the vote was suspended until that inquiry was made.

Half the adult population of Westminster, of course, were not recorded in these sources. Women were excluded from the poll, although they did form part of the election crowds and some famous women acted as political canvassers. Indeed, a number of Whig duchesses became notorious for the enthusiasm of their support for Fox in 1784. That was a source of some heavy-handed humour in the satirical prints.[8] Yet the historical records do also permit the historian some more sober glimpses of the less fashionable female population of Westminster. Above all, a knowledge of the range of male occupations indicates the nature of the local economy and, by inference, the local job opportunities for women. Thus the grand households of the court and aristocrats (in 1790, there were some 150 titled personages in the parish of St George Hanover Square alone)[9] certainly employed large numbers of female servants, as well as the menservants and porters who were entitled to vote. In addition, women worked in the city's many inns

and alehouses; they served in Westminster's dazzling array of
shops, both smart and humble; and women were employed extensively and characteristically in the humdrum employments that
provided basic domestic services outside the home. A striking indicator of female dominance of one key occupation in this sector of
the urban economy was provided by the dauntless James Trotter in
St. George's parish who described himself as a 'laundress' when
casting his vote in 1819.

Moreover, the Westminster records that have been surveyed for
this study do reveal that quite an amount of urban housing was
occupied by women, who paid local rates. Thus it is possible that
some male voters were influenced in their voting, or even acted as
unofficial proxies for these female householders. That certainly
occurred in eighteenth-century Haslemere, a small borough in Sur-
rey which had its own complex freehold franchise. There Miss
Shudd, an attorney's daughter, disposed of five votes which were
cast by local men on her behalf.[10] No political *éminence grise*
among the female property owners in Westminster has yet been
identified. But the more abundant the data available, the greater the
significant details that can emerge. Thus it was revealed in evidence
to a House of Commons enquiry in 1789 that as many as 1,845 or
over 1 in 10 of Westminster's 16,394 inhabited houses were then
headed by women.[11] And that in turn suggests something of the
nature of the local economy and society.

Hence the availability of multiple records allows the historian to
probe beyond the formal election results to search for the community that lived, worked and, on specified occasions, voted in
Westminster. In the chapters that follow we document and describe
the Westminster Historical Database, and we consider in a non-
prescriptive way a number of key issues concerning its effective
usage. Chapter 2 provides the reader with an introduction to Poll
and Rate Books, the two main sources for the Database in its present form. The intention is to convey an authentic feel for the original source material and its provenance.

The location and form of the actual sources used to compile the
Westminster Historical Database are detailed in Chapter 3. It is
explained that the data from poll and rate books are conveniently
held in the form of two-way tables (columns containing data fields
and rows containing records relating to individual people). This is
the standard form for all relational database management systems

(RDBMS), including Oracle and Microsoft Access. A particular virtue of the Database is the ease with which it may readily be imported into virtually all commercially available database management systems.

We take the opportunity in Chapter 3 to sketch out for the reader an overview of political life in the City of Westminster between 1749 and 1820. The aim is to provide enough information for the reader to make effective use of the Database without prejudicing his or her interpretation of events. Of particular importance are the keys given to four sets of codes. The first set of codes provides a ready-made name standardisation facility which simplifies the processes of information retrieval and record linkage. Users of the Database are free to use the built-in nominal codes, or alternatively they may wish to apply their own preferred standardisation algorithms to the original data. The second set of codes is held in the twelve Poll Book tables in the field *Vote*. These codes record the voting patterns of individual electors for each parliamentary election held in Westminster between 1749 and 1820. The codes are derived directly from surviving poll books and are immutable. Likewise, our third set of codes map directly the seven Westminster *Parishes* (and *Wards* in rate book tables) and as such are unchangeable.

Our fourth and final set of codes is of a different order. Occupational Classification remains one of the most controversial topics in historical and social scientific research. In Chapter 4 we consider at some length the problems and purposes of occupational coding schemes. It is suggested that coding is a very necessary evil: without it, empirical testing of relevant hypotheses, theories, or even lowly propositions, is well-nigh impossible. To add significant academic value to the Westminster Historical Database, therefore, there is included a four-level hierarchical classification scheme developed by the authors using the well-known Booth/Armstrong model as a starting point. The coding scheme is sophisticated and sensitive; it may be adopted or adapted by users of the Database. Equally, we recognise that other researchers may have very different needs or viewpoints from our own, leading them to adopt entirely different coding schema. This option is made possible by the retention of the original occupational character strings as a separate field in poll book tables. In other words, by retaining the possibility of post-coding, new users of the Database are freed from interference resulting from the presumptions and inclinations of prior users. This is in accord with the general strategy employed when constructing the Database of minimising the corruption of original sources: we have sought to add value, but not to take it away.

Information Retrieval is the subject of Chapter 5. Our aim is to demonstrate how the Database may be searched with ease using SQL, the standard query language for RDBMS. No attempt is made to provide a comprehensive guide to SQL. Rather, the emphasis is on devising effective search strategies and the development of compound queries which enable the encoding of sophisticated record linkage algorithms.

The availability of query languages with the power and precision of SQL has made possible a revolution in the art of Record Linkage. The nature and logic of this revolution is discussed in Chapter 6. We aim to show how, by developing systematic probabilistic linkage strategies, the potentialities for record linkage and the effective exploitation of the Westminster Historical Database may be maximised. The results of a series of original experiments are reported, and from these stem a number of guidelines for record linkage practice.

In one sense, Chapter 6 is the high point of this book. It offers a practical demonstration of the advances in historical methods made possible through the application of database systems in historical research. More generally, however, our intention in documenting the Westminster Historical Database so thoroughly, and in illustrating its potential for future research, has been to show that the traditional scholarly virtues of verification and careful documentation are just as necessary in the information age as they were in the age of pen and ink. Indeed, they are more so. We have followed in the spirit of Lawrence Stone, who as long ago as 1976 drew attention to the defects of:

> some of the more ambitious of the quantifiers ... their failure to conform to those professional standards, designed to make possible a scientific evaluation of the evidence, which have been built up over a century of painstaking scholarship.[12]

Stone's remedy was to 'deposit all the raw data – the code books, the programmes, and the print-out – in statistical data banks to which serious investigators can go to check through the whole process once again from start to finish'.[13] In offering the Westminster Historical Database to a wider public, we hope not only to have satisfied the strictures of that most eminent of critics, but also to have made generally available a historical resource of enduring value.

*Notes*

[1]   T. Hutchinson (ed.), The poetical works of William Wordsworth (1920), p. 269; J. Wordsworth et al. (eds), William Wordsworth: The Prelude, 1799, 1805, 1850 (New York, 1979), p. 234.

[2]   The pioneering study was M.D. George, *London life in the eighteenth century* (1925; 2nd edn, Harmondsworth, 1966) and see also, for more recent vintage, G. Rudé, *Hanoverian London, 1714-1808* (1971) and L. Schwarz, *London in the age of industrialisation: entrepreneurs, labour force and living conditions, 1700-1850* (Cambridge, 1992).

[3]   For the Westminster scavenger Samuel Collins, see below p. 79.

[4]   See below, p. 34.

[5]   See below, pp. 13-19.

[6]   See E.M. Green, 'The taxonomy of occupations in late eighteenth-century Westminster', in P.J. Corfield and Derek Keene (eds), *Work in towns, 850-1850* (Leicester, 1990), pp. 164-81.

[7]   L. Reid, *Charles James Fox: a man for the people* (1969), p. 208.

[8]   The Duchess of Devonshire was especially pilloried in the public prints for her ardent support for Fox: see e.g. J. Brewer (ed.), *The common people and politics, 1750-90s* (Cambridge, 1986), pp. 206-25: Plates 78-87.

[9]   LMA List of inhabitants of St George, c. 1790, TC/St G/1-2.

[10]  M. Clayton, 'Elections and electioneering in Haslemere, 1715-80' (unpub. M.Phil. thesis, University of London, 1993), pp. 78, 151-2, 185.

[11]  PRO Chatham papers, PRO/30/8/237, fo. 784.

[12]  L. Stone, 'History and the social sciences', in his *The past and the present revisited* (1987), p. 33.

[13]  Ibid., pp. 34-5.

# 2

# Poll and Rate Books

Source-criticism is the essence of scholarship. This takes many forms, from establishing a true text among variants to evaluating the reliability of evidence. This chapter discusses the sources used in the Westminster Historical Database, explaining how poll books and rate books came to exist and to be preserved, and assessing their reliability.

## 2.1 Poll books

Historians of Britain working on the period between the introduction of the ballot in 1872 and the recent rise of public opinion polling must infer political behaviour from aggregated data. Whilst this is far less costly than the collection of individual-level data, there are a number of problems inherent in it. Ballot papers in British parliamentary elections are aggregated within each constituency prior to counting, making the constituency the smallest possible area for spatial or 'ecological' analysis. No social data are included on the ballot papers, and constituencies are not necessarily coterminous with census registration districts for which social data are available.[1]

By contrast, historians working on the period of open voting have in poll books a rich source of individual-level behavioural data.[2] These are the records of voting in parliamentary elections prior to the introduction of the ballot in 1872.[3] They contain the names of the voters and details of the candidates for whom they polled, and may also contain supplementary data such as the address or occupation of the voter, his religious affiliation, his qualification for voting, his tax assessment, or lists of electors who did not poll.[4] They occur in both manuscript and printed form, although historians have generally worked with the latter.[5] There are a number of reasons for this. First, the destruction of the manuscript poll books formerly preserved among the public records at the Crown Office has left many elections recorded only in printed editions. Secondly, printed poll books are legible, complete, and accessible. But not all contested parliamentary elections led to printed poll books. Often poll books for elections in large cities were not printed, presumably because of the costs involved.[6]

The origins of the practice of recording votes remain obscure. Poll lists were made in the early seventeenth century, either as an official record of voting or as evidence to support a petition to the House of Commons in controverted elections. By 1696 a statute required that in county elections:

> In case the said election be not determined upon the view ... but that a poll shall be required for the determination thereof, then the said sheriff ... shall forthwith there proceed to take the said poll ... and ... shall appoint such number of clerks as shall to him seem meet and convenient for taking thereof; which clerks shall all take the said poll ... and to set down the names of each freeholder, and the place of his freehold, and for whom he shall poll. And be it further enacted, that every sheriff, under sheriff, mayor, bailiff, and other officer, to whom the execution of any writ or precept shall belong for the electing members to serve in parliament, shall forthwith deliver to such person or persons, as shall desire the same, a copy of the poll taken at such election, paying only a reasonable charge for writing the same.[7]

Boroughs as well as counties were expected to make poll books. But the statute made no provision for their permanent preservation, although they were crucial evidence in the event of a disputed election. Not until the statute of 1843 was the preservation of borough poll books required.[8] But by then Westminster had already acquired a fine series of electoral records among the muniments of the Westminster Sessions of the Peace. The poll books from the early eighteenth century had already disappeared by 1789.[9] But the series is complete for the period between 1774 and 1820, with the exception of the 1807 election and a number of poll books which have subsequently decayed.[10] Quite possibly the poll books were handed down from one High Bailiff to his successor before finding their last resting place. It has not been possible to trace, or explain the disappearance, of Westminster's manuscript poll book for 1807, and no transcript has yet been found for it.

The first printed poll book in England (from the Essex by-election of 1694) pre-dates the statutory requirement for the taking of polls, and many pre-date the requirement for the preservation of poll books. But the taking of polls rapidly stimulated the appearance of printed editions, of which about 2,200 survive. Historical psephologists have largely relied upon these printed editions, and a number of printed volumes survive for Westminster.[11] Manuscript poll books survive for many Westminster elections for which no printed edition was published, and in compiling the Westminster Historical Database these have been used to provide additional material when appropriate. Yet the completeness of printed poll books gives them advantages over the fragmentary survivals of manuscript poll books, despite potential errors in transcription and typesetting.

English historical psephology owes much to the pioneering work of W.A. Speck who first formulated in relation to the county electorates of the early eighteenth century the questions of behaviour, loyalty, and turnover which continue to dominate the subject.[12] Before this first application of the computer to the discipline, poll books had been used unsystematically for a variety of purposes, including the study of deferential behaviour, the estimation of the size of the electorate, and examination of the social context of political behaviour.[13] Since Speck's initial analysis of poll books, he and others have advanced the methodological frontiers of historical psephology. This has been characterised by a shift from the analysis of a single poll book towards the linkage of two or more sources, using increasingly sophisticated algorithms, to examine the dynamics of political behaviour.[14] This has culminated in O'Gorman's marvellous synthesis of much recent work on the local context of electoral politics, together with an analysis of a wide variety of borough constituencies throughout the Hanoverian period.[15] This reveals how the unreformed electoral system continued to function satisfactorily until the eve of the first Reform Act, and how in many constituencies it satisfied the aspirations and needs of the parties to electoral relationships.

Plate 1 'John Bull in a Quandary' (1788) [George no. 8,361]

Poll books are texts, representations of historical reality that have been transmitted orally at the hustings and by at least two textual processes: of typesetting and data entry, or of data collection and data entry. The imprecise orthography of the poll clerks and compositors leads to renderings such as 'Palm Alley' for 'Pall Mall' or 'German Street' for 'Jermyn Street', and to yet more bizarre spellings of personal names. So the data offered here are related to, but distinct from, the underlying electoral behaviour. As the publisher of the Westminster poll book of 1780 noted in his preface:

> From the noise and confusion of the hustings during the time of taking down the names of the voters, and the expedition in printing a numerous and long-contested poll, like the present, several mistakes must unavoidably have happened, notwithstanding every possible care has been made use of to prevent them.[16]

Some slight differences between election returns and actual political behaviour are apparent, but others must remain forever hidden. These processes of interpretation may be continued by the modern historian's standardisation of the spelling of personal names, by classification of occupations, by use of the parish of residence to represent the place of residence, and by classification of the partisan loyalties of candidates.

In the absence of documents with which the Westminster poll books could be compared, it is difficult to estimate their reliability as evidence. Doubts about the value of poll books are fivefold: first, about the loss or mistranscription of data; secondly, about the extent of fraudulent voting; thirdly, about the value of the occupational descriptions given; fourthly, about the classifications used by historians; and, finally, about the techniques of record linkage employed. But poll books do not suffer from one problem which bedevils much quantitative history: votes were cast to be counted, and the data on voting behaviour were recorded for the purpose for which they may be analysed. And although personation must have occurred, that which escaped the attention of the partisan Inspectors at the hustings must necessarily escape the scrutiny of the historian. In Westminster, these Inspectors were numerous and well-rewarded: in 1774 the agents for Percy and Pelham Clinton employed 15 Inspectors who received £20 each for their services, and another who received £25.[17] In the particularly intense campaigns of the 1780s, the polling of bad votes may have been a matter of policy. George III wrote to Pitt on 13 April 1784 that 'though the advance made by Mr Fox this day can only have been made by bad votes, yet similar measures must be adopted rather than let him get returned for Westminster.'[18]

Nevertheless, the evidence of rejected voters offers some comfort that by and large the Inspectors did their job efficiently. As earlier noted, Fox claimed in the debate on the Westminster scrutiny that individual voters were checked against the parish books, and, in dubious cases, enquiries were made at the putative voter's place of residence to verify or disallow his claim.[19]

Defeated candidates regularly accused their successful rivals of polling unqualified voters: that was part of the stock-in-trade of eighteenth-century electioneering. Such allegations were most frequent in 1788, when Hood's petition to the Commons was a comprehensive indictment of electioneering techniques. It alleged:

> That the returning officer admitted a great number of persons to vote for the said Lord John Townshend, who, by the ancient usage and custom of the said City and Liberty, had no right to vote at the said election, and others who were disqualified from, and incapable by law of, voting at the said election; and that the names of many persons were received upon the poll as voting for Lord John Townshend, who, in fact, did not vote for either of the candidates, but were votes given by other persons, falsely assuming their names and characters, and several persons were admitted to poll more than once at the said election; and that, as well before the said election, as during the time of taking the said poll, many persons, by bribery, gifts, promises of reward, and other undue and illegal practices, did corrupt a great number of the voters to poll at the said election on the part of the said Lord John Townshend.[20]

In the same year, Sir William Young reported to the Marquis of Buckingham that:

> The question is not of title to vote in most cases, but of identity; most families being at this season out of town, a rascal was

found to personate every absentee. The suborners of perjury not regularly conferring, very many instances occur of an absentee being represented by four or five, all admitted to vote on their mere attestation.[21]

But it seems unlikely that rational rascals would knowingly personate someone who had already voted. Instances of identical poll book records are rare, and generally the result of polling by father and son with the same name, address and trade. William Fox, a victualler of George Street in St Margaret and St John, apparently polled three times in 1788, but this is a very rare instance. Finally, it was said that Townshend's canvassers identified empty houses, those occupied by women, and the houses of those who said they would abstain. Strangers were then brought into Westminster from Hoxton and Shoreditch to assume the identities of the occupiers of these houses. These impostors were said to have been taken to houses in Covent Garden, where they were dressed and tutored, before being taken to poll. Others assembled and were victualled at Sheridan's *Theatre Royal* in Drury Lane before creating mayhem at the hustings. For this they were said to have received 5s a day, or £3 if they voted. But it seems unlikely that there were 'very many instances ... of women having voted dressed as men', as Hood's lawyer alleged.[22] Those who convinced the Inspectors of their eligibility to vote must ultimately be accepted as being of equal standing by the historian.

Whilst there remain some problematical areas of the occupations given by the voters, such as the 'yeomen' of 1784, it is found that voters in more than one contest gave broadly consistent occupations. Certainly, the later census authorities in 1891 drew attention to 'the foolish but very common desire of people to magnify the importance of their occupational condition'.[23] This may have occurred in Westminster a century earlier when labourers can sometimes be found being translated into gentlemen in successive elections. But the instances of this are sufficiently uncommon to be remarkable, leading to confidence in the potential use of occupations as one of a number of analytical taxonomies to explain eighteenth-century electoral behaviour.[24]

But before going further, it is important to establish who were the electors in Westminster before 1832, that is, what criteria had to be fulfilled in order to vote, and hence to be included in the

Database. The situation in detail was complicated and provided much work for attorneys specialising in election law; but the general principle became clarified after a series of disputes. At the scrutiny which followed the election of 1749, Peter Leigh the High Bailiff declared the right of voting in Westminster to lie:

> In the inhabitant householders within the said City and Liberty paying or being liable to pay scot and lot, and in the occupiers of chambers in the several Inns in Chancery within the same Liberty, and in the inhabitant householders in Whitehall, Scotland Yard, the Mews and Stable Yard St James's not being the king's menial servants, and in the several watermen belonging to the chest and living in the parishes of St Margaret Westminster or St John the Evangelist or either of them, but nothing in the above opinion is intended to extend to or affect the right of voting for the City and Liberty of Westminster claimed by the inhabitants of St Martin-le-Grand, but such right is left open to future consideration.[25]

But attorneys representing Lord Hood after his defeat in 1789 were unwilling to accept the High Bailiff's declaration. Thomas Corbett, Leigh's successor as High Bailiff, had accepted the votes of householders *liable* to pay scot and lot.[26] 'Paying scot and bearing lot' was itself not readily defined, but it seems to have been accepted as making a contribution towards the parish, most commonly by payment of rates for the maintenance of the poor. However Hood's lawyers contended that the franchise lay in those actually *paying* scot and lot, and that the Duchy of Lancaster estate formed no part of the City and Liberties of Westminster.[27] Eventually a compromise was reached, and in March 1795 the Commons declared the franchise to lie:

> In the inhabitants, householders paying scot and lot, of the united parishes of St Margaret and St John, and of the several parishes of St Paul Covent Garden, St Anne, St James, St George Hanover Square, St Martin-in-the-Fields, St Clement Danes, and St-Mary-le-Strand (including so much and such parts of the said parishes of St Martin-in-the-Fields, St Clement Danes, and St Mary-le-Strand, as are within the liberties, districts, limits, or jurisdictions of the Duchy of Lancaster), and in

the liberty or district of St Martin-le-Grand, in the County of Middlesex, and in the Precinct of the Savoy.[28]

The rule of thumb, then, was that a voter should be a householder, and that 'no person can be deemed to be a householder, who does not possess an exclusive right to the use of the outward door of the building'.[29] Being a householder, whilst necessary, was insufficient to qualify a man to vote in Westminster.[30] As early as 1680 the House of Commons resolved that 'the king's menial servants, not having proper houses of their own within the City of Westminster, have not right to give voices in the election of citizens to serve in parliament for the said city'.[31] And the right of election was further restricted when the Commons declared in 1698 that 'no alien, not being a denizen or naturalised, hath any right to vote in the election of members to serve in parliament.[32] Meanwhile, the tendering of the oath of allegiance at the hustings was designed to exclude 'Papists' from the privilege of voting.

Moreover, the right of voting could change in other ways. In 1789 the Deputy High Bailiff testified before the Commons committee investigating the right of voting in Westminster that 'if the person who claimed the vote had come to reside previous to the *teste* of the writ, I admitted him to vote'.[33] But even as he spoke the Deputy High Bailiff's testimony was out of date, for in 1786 legislation had been enacted requiring that voters in borough constituencies should be resident for six months prior to the election.[34]

Not even the old chestnut of payment of rates was immune to change. In 1820 the case of Cullen *v.* Morris was tried in the court of King's Bench before Lord Chief Justice Abbott. Cullen had been in arrears with his rates when he sought to vote in 1819, and he was rejected by Arthur Morris, the High Bailiff. So Cullen left and paid off his arrears, and on returning he was again rejected. The Lord Chief Justice gave his opinion that, as no demand for rates had been made of Cullen in person, then he did indeed have the right to vote. So in 1820 householders were rejected only if they had refused to pay their rates.[35] Since the collection of rates might be made as infrequently as once a year, and the residence requirement even after 1786 was only six months' residence, this gave considerable scope for voting by those who had not paid their rates. Moreover, those who had moved within the constituency during the six months prior to an election, having previously paid their rates elsewhere in the constituency and continuing to be liable to pay rates, were also entitled to vote although their names would not be found in the rate books at the address they gave to the poll clerk.

Some anomalous groups of non-householders or non-ratepayers were specifically mentioned in the High Bailiff's declaration of the franchise in 1749 as having the right to vote. These included first, 'the occupiers of chambers in the several Inns in Chancery', who were not householders and whose rates were paid collectively by their Inn. Secondly were included 'the inhabitant householders in Whitehall, Scotland Yard, the Mews and Stable Yard St James's' who occupied parts of the royal palaces. Thirdly were included 'the several watermen belonging to the chest', who were beneficiaries of a charity for aged and infirm watermen supported by tolls on the Sunday ferry made after the building of Westminster Bridge, and who made no claims upon the parish rates. In practice, none of these groups was numerous. There was also an anomalous area, the Liberty of St Martin-le-Grand, which lay within the City of London, and a disputed area, the estates of the Duchy of Lancaster and the Liberty of the Savoy, which lay in the eastern part of the parish of St Clement Danes, predominantly between the Strand and the river Thames. One final anomaly, not mentioned by the High Bailiff in 1749, will conclude this discussion of who was eligible for inclusion in the Database. Thomas Corbett testified in 1789 that he permitted partners in trade to vote if they were residents, although they did not have to be resident householders.[36] In 1749 John Scott was a brewer in St Margaret's parish, where he lived and where he shared a brewery with John Searanche. Searanche was not a householder, but voted by virtue of the rates he paid on the brewery.[37] According to Bickersteth:

If a house occupied by a firm be rated in the names of A.B. and C.D., both A.B. and C.D. are entitled to vote; if it be rated in the names of A.B. and sons, then A.B. and his sons are all of them entitled to vote; but if it be rated in the names of A.B. and Co., A.B. only is entitled to vote.[38]

Plate 2 'The Devonshire Method to Restore a Lost Member' (1784) [George no. 6,530]

In his evidence before the Select Committee on Polls in 1827, Francis Place described how elections were conducted:

> When a man comes to poll, he gives his name in, and as soon as he gives his name, the person who holds the rate books looks to see if the name of that person is in the book, if he does not know him personally, which is very likely to be the case; and the man that holds the collecting book then looks to see if the rate is paid up; and if the name appears, and the last collection is paid, he is permitted to vote.[39]

In practice, however, things were never so clear-cut as these neat definitions suggested.

Some people undoubtedly voted who were not strictly qualified to do so. Problems in determining just who was eligible to vote were exacerbated because of disorder at the elections. For many people, elections had a carnivalesque quality.[40] The mixture of alcohol, crowds, and partisan loyalty meant that the environs of the hustings in Covent Garden were rowdy and occasionally dangerous. In 1741 this led to a suspension of polling when the mob 'threw into the portico dirt, stones, sticks, dead cats and dogs, so that the candidates, High Bailiff, clerks and Inspectors were obliged to retire into the church'.[41] In these circumstances protestations that the name of each voter was checked in the parish books must be taken with a pinch of salt.

Nor was it possible in such circumstances to exclude from the poll all 'Papists', paupers and aliens. It was hard to tell if a man was an alien, for example, and his accent, dress, habits, and reputation were all liable to be taken into consideration. Peter Harris, a chandler of Wardour Street in St Anne's parish, was widely believed to be a foreigner. One witness told the scrutiny after the election of 1749 that Harris 'said he was an Englishman, but he spoke like a Dutchman with a foreign accent like the people of Amsterdam ... I could tell by his hair and his Dutch coat that he was a Dutchman'. Another witness stated that 'he has the Dutch accent strongly, and by that and the smoking his pipe I believe him to be a Dutchman. It is the common repute of the neighbourhood that he is a Dutchman'.[42] Nevertheless, Harris had successfully voted.

Whilst the process of checking on the *bona fides* of would-be voters was clearly not as scrupulous as its defenders claimed, it was equally clearly not so negligent as its detractors maintained. Considerable efforts were made to ensure that only qualified electors could vote: many individuals were sent by the Inspectors for more careful questioning by the High Bailiff; and from this more careful questioning few returned to poll. Whilst necessarily bearing in mind the caveats noted above, the Westminster poll books may be used as a proxy for a population consisting of the constituency's adult male householders. Moreover, the data on voting behaviour are incomparably robust by the standards of the eighteenth and nineteenth centuries. Here we have direct evidence of mass behaviour which may be used for the purpose for which it was recorded.[43] For votes were cast for no other reason than that they should be counted.

## 2.2 Rate books

From at least the beginning of the seventeenth century until 1990, English local government was financed, in whole or in part, by a variety of levies on property colloquially known as 'the rates'.[44] In late eighteenth-century Westminster this levy of a proportion of the assessed annual value of immovable property was generally paid by the occupiers to make provision for welfare (the poor rate), for rudimentary public health (the sewers and the scavenger), for a measure of security (lighting and the Watch), and for the maintenance of the highways. Parish officers levied an amount at a given rate on the assessed annual value or rack rent of each property within their jurisdiction. The rates were collected from the occupiers of property at intervals varying between once a quarter and once a year.[45] The data collected usually consist of the names and addresses of the occupiers together with the rack rental valuations of the properties. In its current form, the Westminster Historical Database does not contain data relating to the rate at which the impost was levied, nor of the sums collected and the frequency of collection.

Rack rent data were entered into the Westminster Historical Database because of the problem of inferring social classification from occupations. For whilst the nominal data of occupations do not fall into a hierarchy, the numerical data of the rate books are easily ranked, representing the relative value of property occupied by the voters.[46] Poll books show the occupations of almost all Westminster's voters, but rack rent valuations can only be found for some of them. The proportion depends upon the linkage algorithm adopted, but it is typically between two-fifths and three-fifths of those poll book records offered for linkage. Both poll books and rate books are valuable for social and economic classification, and in combination their value is enhanced. But rate books are a more intractable source than poll books, and even the devoted Edwin Cannan described his subject as 'dry' and 'odious'.[47]

The linkage of poll and rate books is discussed in greater detail in Chapter 6.3 below. The problem is complicated, but in essence it revolves around the key fact that there are many ways by which poll and rate books may be linked, and that implementing different linkage criteria will produce different results. Poll books and rate books may contain common character strings in the fields representing *Name* and *Place* of residence. A simple linkage algorithm may be implemented linking poll and rate book tables on the criterion of having common character strings in the fields *Surname*, *Shtname*, *Parish* and *Street* which would link data for about a third of the poll book cases. However, sequential implementation of multiple pass record linkage algorithms using successively weaker linkage criteria would link data for substantially more poll book cases.

Typically, the rate books in Westminster were set out in a street-by-street perambulation adopted by the rate collectors. This seems to have changed little during the period under discussion. Within any one street the rate book was set out in this format (other columns indicated the amount of rate collected, any arrears, and the comments of the rate collectors such as 'exceedingly insolent and refused to pay' and 'indigent and excused payment').

Doubts may be raised about the evidential value of rack rent assessments in illuminating political behaviour. These doubts fall into two groups: first, considering the rates themselves; and, secondly, concerning the algorithm used to link assessments and poll books. But the values imputed to properties broadly reflect the size and quality of the accommodation. To take an example, Goodwin's Court in St Martin's parish contains some of the smallest houses in Westminster to have survived from the eighteenth century. These properties are on three storeys, but have only a single room on each

storey connected by a small staircase. In 1784, the six houses in the
narrow court recorded rateable values ranging from £6 to £18, with
a mean of £11.50.[48] By contrast, the houses in Meard Street in St
Anne's parish were rather larger than those in Goodwin's Court,
although they were situated in a small street. These seven houses in
1784 had values ranging from £32 to £40, with a mean of £35.33.
Unlike the houses in Goodwin's court, those in Meard Street had
two rooms on each of four storeys.[49] Finally, the splendid house in
Soho Square at the end of Greek Street was extensively refurbished
by Richard Beckford in 1754, whereupon its rack rent was doubled
to £240.[50] It is evident that rack rent values broadly reflected the
size and location of the property. Moreover, the variations in detail
which inevitably occurred in the comparison of individual cases
should be lost in the aggregation of all cases.

**Table 2.1 Specimen of rate book data (£)**

Greek Street, west side beginning at Compton Street

| Name | Rack rent |
| --- | --- |
| William Grant | 52 |
| Empty | 27 |
| Joseph Creswell | 27 |
| Elizabeth Barrett | 16 |
| Thomas Hamilton | 32 |
| Sachell | 50 |

Source: WAC A/326.

Contemporaries differed as to whether Westminster's franchise
lay in the ratepayers or in those 'liable to pay' rates.[51] Given the
High Bailiff's testimony before the House of Commons in 1789
that he had followed precedent in admitting to vote 'inhabitant
householders paying or liable to pay scot and lot', and that he
'considered a man being rated as proof of his being a householder',[52] together with Fox's assertion that 'each voter's name,
profession, and description [were] collated with the [parish]
books',[53] a high degree of correspondence between the poll books
and the rate books might be expected.
    Yet when linked (by list-unique surname, standardised forename,

and parish and street of residence), rate data could only be found
for about one third of the voters in 1784. Some of those who
polled but who cannot be traced in the rate books must have been
fraudulent voters, but it is striking just how few voters were rejected in the scrutiny which followed the election of 1784. More
likely causes of the disparity between the two sources were: the
mobility of voters (those who had paid rates in one parish were
entitled to vote in the parish to which they moved, even if they had
not been resident there for the required six months); the voting of
business partners; the apparent toleration of voting by one member
of a household when the rates were paid by another; the fact that
often the rate books recorded only the surname of the householder;
non-list-unique rate book entries; the fact that voters sometimes
gave a different address within a parish from that recorded in the
rate books; and perhaps most importantly of all, simple errors or
mis-spellings in one or both of the sources.

Working in haste, neither the parish officers nor the poll clerks
were concerned to establish the identity of householders to the
standards of accuracy sought by the historian; and such checks
which were made in the rate books as to a man's eligibility to poll
were made independently of the record in the poll book. If levels of
record linkage are inversely related to confidence in the linkages
achieved, then disappointing linkage levels between poll books and
rate books are as much a reflection of confidence that a tight linkage algorithm will make a high proportion of true links, as a *prima
facie* case that either source is fundamentally flawed.[54] In any case,
historical research is not a competition to see who can link the
highest proportion of records.

In addition, the work of Elizabeth Baigent on incomplete records of parish rates in late eighteenth-century Bristol has cast doubt
on the comparability of different rating sources.[55] Her attempt to
infer rack rent values of properties from known rateable values
found that there was a low correlation between the values recorded
in different sets of local rate data. In part this reflects the objectives
of her study, which concerned the handling by computer of fragmentary historical sources. In a matrix of rated properties and a
number of different rate assessments in Bristol, complete data
existed for only a quarter of the properties. Baigent estimated the
values of the missing cells on the basis: firstly of those cells for
which data were present, and secondly on the basis of the results of

the first process, including estimated results. In her final file, over half of the entries were estimated using real data, and a fifth were estimated using real and estimated data. But the phenomenon of wide variations in assessments for the same property for different local rates has not been found for Westminster in the period. Whilst little attempt has been made to compare rack rent valuations taken from different rates, the Westminster data are complete. Rack rent values for given properties appear to be similar, whilst there is a high correlation with the amounts charged under the Land Tax, as the following example of a selection of rack rent assessments and the Land Tax from Greek Street in 1784 suggests.

**Table 2.2 Comparison of different rate assessments in Westminster (£)**

Greek Street, west side

| Name | Poor Rate | Watch Rate | Land Tax |
|------|-----------|------------|----------|
| Grant | 52 | 52 | 32 |
| Creswell | 27 | 27 | 15 |
| Barrett | 16 | 16 | 10 |
| Hamilton | 32 | 32 | 8 |
| Sachell | 50 | 50 | 33 |
| Dickenson | 40 | 40 | 25 |
| Mill | 36 | 36 | 24 |
| Empty | 32 | 32 | 25 |
| Addington | 56 | 56 | 35 |
| Ford | 48 | 48 | 33 |
| Fowler | 40 | 40 | 25 |

Source: WAC A/326; A/1565; A/1796.

It will be noted that the rack rent valuations in the Poor Rate and Watch Rate assessments are identical. In a test of the correlation between rack rent and Land Tax assessments for 45 houses in Greek Street, the correlation coefficient was 0.97.[56] This similarity does not lead to any greater confidence in the use of any one rate, but it suggests that the valuations shared a common source. This is important, because although the Poor Rate assessment has been used where possible, when it was unavailable another rate book (generally the Watch Rate) was used instead. The Land Tax assessments were not used, as these were said to be derived from the Poor Rate. Thus the rate data may be seen to offer a hierarchical classification of a sample of Westminster voters, on a consistent basis, using a contemporary measure that (for all the perennial complaints about local government rates) was accepted by the voters themselves.

The value of the rates as an historical source may be disputed. Old assessments, and allegations of corruption on the part of the rating authorities, are alleged to leave the source at least tainted and possibly worthless. But a pilot study of the Westminster sources showed that in the case of the status titles of the voters from the united parishes of St Margaret and St John in 1784, which fall more naturally into a hierarchy than do the majority of voters' occupations, the mean rack rent assessments for various groups showed a plausible distribution.[57] These status titles relate to those voters who were described as 'gentlemen', 'esquires' and so on, and were classified 'RE' in the occupational classification.

**Table 2.3 Average assessments of property of identified rate-paying status-givers in St Margaret and St John, 1784 (£)**

| Status | Mean | Median | Cases |
|---|---|---|---|
| Titled nobility | 150 | 150 | 1 |
| Knights and baronets | 107 | 85 | 6 |
| Esquires | 57 | 45 | 69 |
| Gentlemen | 21 | 15 | 173 |
| All status-givers | 34 | 23 | 249 |

Source: Green, 'Taxonomy of occupations', in Corfield and Keene (eds), *Work in towns*, p. 174.

The amount actually paid in rates was the product of a number of factors, including the rack rent value of the property, the rate in the pound levied, and the frequency of collection. Because the rates were collected to finance local needs, there is no reason to suppose that the sums collected were comparable on a parish-by-parish basis. The amount of rate collected was likely to reflect the demand for services for which the rate was levied as much as ability to pay. Hence, as noted above, the Westminster Historical Database, as currently constituted, has tabulated rack rent assessments throughout, while ignoring the sums actually paid.

The rack rent valuations contained in the rate books are no more than an approximation to the relative standing of Westminster's householders. But they are nonetheless of value. Close examination of the original rate books reveals shifts in the valuation of individual properties relative to neighbouring properties over time, suggesting that new valuations were made in response to changing circumstances. Moreover, householders who felt that their assessments were excessive might appeal to the rating authorities, in response to which the assessment might be revised slightly: in such cases it is the new assessment which has been incorporated into the Database. Accuracy of rack rent valuations relative to neighbours is likely to have been high as individuals contested what they believed to be unreasonable valuations. It is thus likely that the rateable value of a house reflected broadly the ability of the householder to pay the rates, because the rates would have been a secondary criterion after the rent in deciding where to live.

Historians are trained in the skills of making provisional conclusions on the basis of partial, biased, incomplete, fragmentary and Janus-faced evidence, whilst allowing for contingent factors such as the luck of sources having been created and of having survived and the serendipity of their having been found. Neither poll books nor rate books lie without these general considerations. And yet for all the problematic nature of their sources, historians must offer conclusions or they must starve. No systematic data survive for the income of Westminster's eighteenth-century voters; and the nominal data of occupations, whilst valuable for some purposes, is of limited value for creating or inferring a social hierarchy. We believe that the rack rent valuations contained in the rate book tables may serve as a proxy for income and as a measure of social standing.

Rate books therefore add to the problems as well as the potentialities for historians. In the case of Westminster, there seems to have been one main rating assessment that was used for all local taxation (unlike the multiplicity of local rates used in Bristol). Hence the Westminster rate books have been used in conjunction with the poll books to create the Westminster Historical Database whose details are explained below in Chapter 3.

*Notes*

1   Constituencies were grouped into yet larger units to correspond with census registration districts in K.D. Wald, *Crosses on the ballot: patterns of British voter alignment since 1885* (Princeton, 1983).

2   Open voting was customary in parts of the United States in the early nineteenth century, and persisted in Denmark until 1901. See P. Bourke and D. DeBats, 'Identifiable voting in nineteenth-century America: toward a comparison of Britain and the United States before the secret ballot', *Perspectives in American History*, 11 (1978), pp. 259-88; A.G. Bogue, 'The quest for numeracy: data and methods in American political history', *Journal of Interdisciplinary History*, 21 (1990), pp. 89-116; and J. Elklit, 'Nominal record linkage and the study of non-secret voting: a Danish case', *Journal of Interdisciplinary History*, 15 (1985), pp. 419-43.

3   35 & 36 Victoria c. 33, An Act to amend the law relating to procedure at parliamentary and municipal elections. Since the ballot is necessarily secret the familiar expression 'secret ballot' is a pleonasm. *O.E.D., s.v.* 'Ballot'.

4   J.M. Sims (ed.), *A handlist of British parliamentary poll books* (Leicester, 1984); and J. Gibson and C. Rogers (eds.), *Poll books: c. 1696-1872: a directory of holdings in Great Britain* (3rd edn, Birmingham, 1994). Another Westminster poll book for 1749 was not noticed by Sims: Anon., *A list of persons who, by the poll taken at the late election of a citizen to serve in parliament for the City and Liberty of Westminster, appear to have voted for the Right Hon. Lord Visc. Trentham, as entered in the book opened for the parish of St Martin* [1749].

5   J.A. Phillips, *Electoral behavior in unreformed England: plumpers, splitters and straights* (Princeton, 1982), p. 328, reported supplementing a *lacuna* among the printed poll books for Maidstone with a manuscript. The manuscript poll book of the Yorkshire election of 1734 was analysed by P. Adman, W.A. Speck and B. White in an appendix to J.F. Quinn, 'Yorkshiremen go to the polls: county contests in the early eighteenth century', *Northern History*, 21 (1985), pp. 137-74. Manuscript poll books were used in D. Hirst and S. Bowler, 'Voting in Hertford, 1679-1721', *History and Computing*, 1 (1989), pp. 14-18.

6   Printed poll books in large constituencies were expensive. The Westminster poll books of 1749 and 1774 were priced at 2s 6d, whilst a publisher's advertisement for the 1818 poll book offered the work in

eight parts at 1s each. Anon., 'A collection of addresses, pamphlets, posters, squibs, etc. relating to the Westminster election, 1818' (Bound ephemera in BL). Poll books were a minority taste, and print runs were probably small.

[7] 7 & 8 William III c. 25, An Act for the further regulating elections of members to serve in parliament, and for the preventing irregular proceedings of sheriffs, and other officers, in the electing and returning such members.

[8] 6 & 7 Victoria c. 18, An Act to amend the law for the registration of persons entitled to vote, and to define certain rights of voting, and to regulate certain proceedings in the election of members to serve in parliament for England and Wales.

[9] PRO 30/8/237, fo. 791.

[10] LMA Westminster poll books, WR/PP.

[11] Anon., *Copy of the poll for a citizen for the City and Liberty of Westminster* (1749); Anon., *A correct copy of the poll for electing two representatives for the City and Liberty of Westminster* (1774); Anon., *Copy of the poll for the election of two citizens to serve in the present parliament for the City and Liberty of Westminster* (1780); Anon., *The poll book, for electing two representatives in parliament for the City and Liberty of Westminster* (1818).

[12] W.A. Speck and W.A. Gray, 'Computer analysis of poll books: an initial report', *Bulletin of the Institute of Historical Research*, 43 (1970), pp. 105-12; and W.A. Speck, W.A. Gray and R. Hopkinson, 'Computer analysis of poll books: a further report', *Bulletin of the Institute of Historical Research*, 48 (1975), pp. 64-90.

[13] D.C. Moore, 'The other face of reform', *Victorian Studies*, 5 (1961), pp. 7-34; J.H. Plumb, 'The growth of the electorate in England, 1600-1715', *Past and Present*, 45 (1969), pp. 90-116; G. Rudé, 'The Middlesex electors of 1768-9', *English Historical Review*, 75 (1960), pp. 601-17; and J.R. Vincent, *Poll books: how Victorians voted* (Cambridge, 1967).

[14] J.C. Mitchell and J. Cornford, 'The political demography of Cambridge, 1832-68', *Albion*, 9 (1977), pp. 242-72; and Phillips, *Electoral behavior*.

[15] F. O'Gorman, *Voters, patrons, and parties: the unreformed electoral system of Hanoverian England, 1734-1832* (Oxford, 1989).

[16] Anon., *Copy of the poll ... for the City and Liberty of Westminster* (1780). The publisher's advertisement is on the *verso* of the title-page. Thomas Cornwall testified in 1789 that forty years before 'they made

a misentry with regard to my occupation ... they called me carpenter instead of apothecary'. PRO 30/8/237, fo. 910.

[17] BL Add. MS 33,123, fo. 119.

[18] Cited in L.G. Mitchell, *Charles James Fox* (Oxford, 1992), p. 70.

[19] See above, p. 3.

[20] *House of Commons Journals*, xliv, p. 125. An election print (George, no. 7,363) entitled 'Six voters made out of one, in favour of Lord John Townshend' showed one man in six different disguises. George, vi, p. 519. George also cites an advertisement pasted to the print in the BM Department of Prints and Drawings, offering for sale 'all the curious and valuable wardrobe, in which all the various voters masqueraded at the last election for Lord John Townshend'.

[21] R. Grenville, *Memoirs of the court and cabinets of George III* (4 vols, 1853-5), i, p. 418.

[22] PRO 30/8/237, fo. 785.

[23] Cited in W.A. Armstrong, 'The use of information about occupation' in E.A. Wrigley (ed.), *Nineteenth-century society: essays in the use of quantitative methods for the study of social data* (Cambridge, 1972), p. 210.

[24] For techniques and problems of classifying historical occupations, see Chapter 4, passim.

[25] BL Lansdowne MS 509a, fo. 106.

[26] PRO 30/8/237, fos. 790-96.

[27] PRO 30/8/237, fo. 811.

[28] *House of Commons Journals*, l, p. 339. This was cited in 51 George III c. 126, An act to extend an act made in the eighteenth year of his late majesty King George II, to explain and amend the laws touching the election of knights of the shire to serve in parliament for England, respecting the expenses of hustings and poll clerks, so far as regards the City of Westminster. See Green, 'Thesis' for further details of Westminster's fluid franchise in the period.

[29] Anon., *Disqualifications for voting*, p. 3, in Anon., 'A collection of addresses, pamphlets, posters, squibs, etc. relating to the Westminster election, 1818' (Bound ephemera in BL).

[30] The use of the male form is intentional. John Simeon's *Treatise on the law of elections, in all its branches* (1789), p. 50, declared that the right of voting in parliamentary elections was 'the much-admired and envied liberty of an Englishman. Women, infants, idiots, and madmen are absolutely disqualified from the exercise of this privilege'.

[31] *House of Commons Journals*, ix, p. 654.

[32] *House of Commons Journals*, xii, p. 367.

33    PRO 30/8/237, fo. 926.

34    26 George III c. 100, An act to prevent occasional inhabitants from
      voting in the election of members to serve in parliament, for cities and
      boroughs, in that part of Great Britain called England, and in the
      dominion of Wales.

35    This outline of the case is taken from Anon., *Report of the trial of the
      cause between John Cullen, plaintiff, and Arthur Morris, defendant,
      for refusing to receive the plaintiff's vote at the election for a Member
      of Parliament for the City of Westminster* (1820).

36    PRO 30/8/237, fo. 794.

37    PRO 30/8/237, fo. 800.

38    BL Add. MS 27,843, fo. 64.

39    *B.P.P.* (1826-7), iv, p. 1123.

40    M. Harrison, *Crowds and history: mass phenomena in English towns,
      1790-1835* (Cambridge, 1988), pp. 202-33. Thus George Lamb was
      almost inaudible when he tried to address the electors from the hust-
      ings in 1819 because of the incessant baaing of the crowd. BL
      Broughton papers, Add. MS 56,540, fo. 55.

41    BL Speeches and other collections relating to parliament, Stowe MS
      354, fo. 243.

42    BL Lansdowne MS 509a, fos. 286-7.

43    The only comparable source is the Division Lists of the House of
      Commons. These have the advantage of being surveys of an elite
      group, which should reduce record linkage problems, but the disad-
      vantage of deriving from unofficial sources which may be incomplete.
      See D.E. Ginter (ed.), *Voting records of the British House of Com-
      mons, 1661-1820* (6 vols, 1995).

44    On parish rates in general, see E. Cannan, *History of local rates in
      England* (1896), and J.V. Beckett, *Local taxation: national legislation
      and the problem of enforcement* (1980).

45    Occasionally landlords would pay the rates of properties that had been
      divided into tenements, and add a corresponding amount to the rent.

46    Perhaps because of the refractory nature of the source, rate books have
      been little used by historical psephologists. Phillips, *Electoral behav-
      ior*, pp. 273-4, used Land Tax registers for Norwich and Maidstone,
      but found tax assessments for only about 15 per cent of the Norwich
      voters. However N. Rogers, *Whigs and cities: popular politics in the
      age of Walpole and Pitt* (Oxford, 1989), p. 330, reported finding tax
      data for 19.5 per cent of Norwich voters in 1734 and 28.4 per cent of
      Norwich voters in 1710. The use of parish rate data was suggested by
      M. Drake (ed.), *Introduction to historical psephology* (Milton Keynes,

1982). Parish rates were also used in Mitchell and Cornford 'The political demography of Cambridge'; and in R.S. Neale, 'Class conflict and the poll books in Victorian England', in idem, *Class and ideology in the nineteenth century* (1972), pp. 62-74.

[47]  Cannan, *History of local rates in England*, p. 1.

[48]  G. Gates and W.H. Godfrey (eds.), *Survey of London, xx, The parish of St Martin-in-the-Fields* (1940), p. 108. The mean rack rent of all the houses in St Martin occupied by voters was £24.99. The mean for Goodwin's Court was thus less than half of that for the parish as a whole.

[49]  F.H.W. Sheppard (ed.), *Survey of London, xxiii, The parish of St Anne Soho* (1966), pp. 241-6. The mean rack rent of all the houses in St Anne occupied by voters was £30.82.

[50]  Ibid., pp. 88-105.

[51]  See Green, 'Thesis' for further details of the franchise.

[52]  PRO 30/8/237, fos. 790-6.

[53]  Cited in Reid, *Charles James Fox*, p. 208.

[54]  Linkage strategies for the Westminster data set are discussed in C. Harvey and E.M. Green, 'Record linkage algorithms: efficiency, selection and relative confidence', *History and Computing*, 6 (1994), pp. 143-52, and in C. Harvey, E.M. Green and P.J. Corfield, 'Record linkage theory and practice: an experiment in the application of multiple pass linkage algorithms', *History and Computing*, 8 (1996), pp. 78-89.

[55]  E. Baigent, 'Assessed taxes as sources for the study of urban wealth: Bristol in the late eighteenth century', *Urban History Yearbook 1988* (Leicester, 1988), pp. 31-48; and idem, 'Economy and society in eighteenth-century English towns: Bristol in the 1770s', in D. Denecke and G. Shaw (eds.), *Urban historical geography: recent progress in Britain and Germany* (Cambridge, 1988), pp. 109-24.

[56]  WAC St Anne Poor Rate (1784), A/326; St Anne Watch Rate (1784), A/1565; and St Anne Land Tax (1784), A/1796.

[57]  Green, 'Taxonomy of occupations', p. 174. This pilot study used hand-linked data, dependent essentially upon common strings for standardised surname and standardised forename, but allowing minor variations of address within the parish.

# 3

# The Westminster Historical Database

The historical data contained in the Westminster Historical Database are held in two kinds of tables, distinguished by their names as Poll Book tables (prefix **P**) and Rate Book tables (prefix **R**). Supplementary data are held in a **Dictionary** table and a **Sounds** table. A summary of these tables is shown below in Figure 3.1; they are described in further detail in later sections of this chapter.

**Figure 3.1 Summary of the content and structure of the Westminster Historical Database**

| | |
|---|---:|
| **Poll Books** | |
| Number of database tables | 12 |
| Number of fields per table | 14 |
| Average number of records per table | 7,284 |
| Total number of poll book records | 87,410 |
| | |
| **Rate Books** | |
| Number of database tables | 9 |
| Number of  fields per table | 10 |
| Average number of records per table | 6,270 |
| Total number of rate book records | 56,430 |
| | |
| **Dictionary of Occupations and related codes** | |
| Number of database tables | 1 |
| Number of fields per table | 5 |
| Total number of occupational records | 2,156 |
| | |
| **Dictionary of Surnames and related Soundex codes** | |
| Number of database tables | 1 |
| Number of fields per table | 2 |
| Total number of surname records | 23,558 |

## Figure 3.2 Structure of the Westminster Historical Database

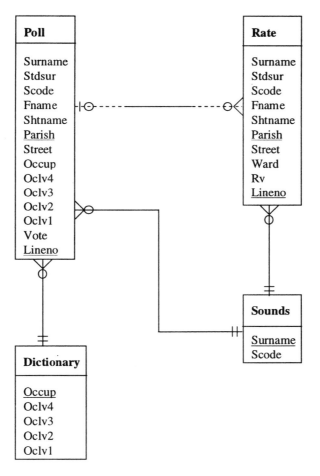

Notes: Most relationships between the entities shown are 1 to many (1:*n*). This is shown by a solid line linking two related entities; a crow's foot indicates the 'many' side of the relationship and a single bar across the line indicates the 'one' side of the relationship.

Further symbols are used to indicate the cardinality of the relationship: either 0 or 1. The relationship between Dictionary and Poll indicates that for every entry in the Dictionary table there may be 0 or many entries in a particular Poll table, and that for every entry in a Poll table there must be one and only one entry in the Dictionary table. The broken line at either end of the relationship between Poll and Rate tables shows that a record in a Poll table may, but need not, be attached to a record in a Rate table, or *vice versa*. The primary key field(s) in each table are underlined.

## 3.1 Poll book tables

Poll book tables exist for each of the twelve contested parliamentary elections from the period 1749 to 1820 for which Westminster
data survive. The total number of records in poll book tables is
87,410. The short name of each table identifies it as holding poll
book data and the year in which the election took place.

Poll book data have been taken from both manuscript and
printed poll books. Many of the former are incomplete, whilst the
latter have been through processes of transcription and typesetting
during which changes may have been made. If a printed poll book
exists, then this has been used as the source of data; if no printed
poll book exists, then the data derive from manuscript sources. The
exception to this general rule is **P1780**. The printed poll book for
1780 lacks occupational data, whilst the manuscript poll books are
complete for the parishes of St Anne and St Margaret and St John.
So in **P1780** data for these two parishes are drawn from the manuscript rather than the printed poll book.

**Table 3.1 Poll book tables in the Westminster Historical Database**

| Table Name | Description | Number of Records |
|---|---|---|
| **P1749** | Poll book data, by-election of 1749 | 9,463 |
| **P1774** | Poll book data, general election of 1774 | 7,514 |
| **P1780** | Poll book data, general election of 1780 | 9,134 |
| **P1784** | Poll book data, general election of 1784 | 11,427 |
| **P1788** | Poll book data, by-election of 1788 | 8,226 |
| **P1790** | Poll book data, general election of 1790 | 5,015 |
| **P1796** | Poll book data, general election of 1796 | 3,058 |
| **P1802** | Poll book data, general election of 1802 | 4,682 |
| **P1806** | Poll book data, general election of 1806 | 4,611 |
| **P1818** | Poll book data, general election of 1818 | 10,138 |
| **P1819** | Poll book data, by-election of 1819 | 6,556 |
| **P1820** | Poll book data, general election of 1820 | 7,586 |
| **Total** | | **87,410** |

In the poll book tables discussed below, the tables **P1749**,
**P1774**, **P1780** and **P1818** are drawn from printed poll books, and
may be taken as surveys of the voting population of Westminster.

The other tables are drawn from manuscript poll books, and with the exception of **P1802** all suffer some *lacunae*. Manuscript poll books were created at elections for each parish (or grouped parishes) in the constituency; hence the loss of data ranges from the loss of part of the records for a parish in a single election, to the loss of all the data from one or more parishes at one or more elections.

Poll book tables are laid out in a standard format reflecting the structure of the source. Printed poll books for Westminster record the surname and forename of each voter, together with information about his place of residence. This generally consisted of the parish and street of residence, but in 1818 it also included the number within the street of the voter's house. This house number has not been included in the Westminster Historical Database. An occupation or status was generally given for each voter in the printed poll books, although this information was left out of the printed poll book for 1780. Finally, and crucially, printed poll books record the candidate or candidates for whom each voter polled.

Manuscript poll books record all the information contained in the printed poll books, together with supplementary information which has not been included in the Database. This supplementary information includes the date on which the voter polled, the sequence in which voters polled within any one manuscript book, and an indication against the names of voters sharing a common forename and surname combination (generally voting consecutively from the same address if they were father and son) that one was 'senior' and one was 'junior'. Other supplementary information to be found in the manuscript poll books include an indication that the voter swore the oaths required of him, that the oaths were not required of him, or that (being a Quaker) he affirmed in lieu of swearing the oaths. Manuscript poll books also indicate whether, and often on what grounds, an elector was challenged at the hustings, and by the nineteenth century they frequently record the number of a voter's house within his street of residence. Further information recorded on a less systematic basis included the names of public houses occupied by victuallers, and the laconic entries of the poll clerks of the would-be voters who 'ran away when challenged' or were 'too drunk to vote'. None of this information has been included in the poll book tables, which contain only successful acts of voting: that is, would-be voters who were challenged at the hustings and who cast no vote are excluded.

Poll book tables record the surname (*Surname*) and forename (*Fname*) of each voter, together with his parish (*Parish*) and street (*Street*) of residence, the occupation or status given (*Occup*), and the candidate or candidates for whom he polled (*Vote*). Further data are generated from these fields. These include two surname standardisation routines, *Stdsur* and *Scode* (the latter from the table **Sounds**), and a forename standardisation routine *Shtname*. From *Occup* is derived a four-level occupational code contained in the table **Dictionary**. The four levels of the occupational code are *Oclv1*, *Oclv2*, *Oclv3* and *Oclv4*. Finally, poll book tables contain line numbers (*Lineno*) which were entered sequentially during data entry. Data were entered sequentially for each parish, and the combination of *Parish* and *Lineno* identifies each record uniquely within a **Table**. Because of the data validation process, not all line numbers within the range available have been utilised.

The fields *Surname*, *Fname* and *Occup* contain data in character form replicating the character strings for each of these fields in the source. The field *Parish* contains a single character encoding data identifying the voter's parish of residence. Parish codes for poll book tables are shown in Table 3.17 below.

The field *Street* has been subjected to minor standardisation from the character string recorded in the source material. In the first place house numbers within a street have been eliminated as inconsistent and unreliable. For the same reason address qualifiers were eliminated, so that both Great and Little St Anne's Lane were entered as 'ST ANNES LA', both Old and New Bond Street were entered as 'BOND ST', both Upper and Lower St Martin's Lane were entered as 'ST MARTINS LA', and so on. It will be noted that the apostrophe was not entered. Supplementary information in the address field was also excluded, such as the names of public houses and locations within a major named thoroughfare such as 'near the church'. Also excluded were the names of villages such as 'Pimlico' and 'Chelsea', although addresses followed by the identifiers 'Kensington' and 'Knightsbridge' were standardised to the names of those villages.

## Table 3.2 Standard format for poll book tables

| Field Name | Description | Data Type | Field Length |
|---|---|---|---|
| Surname | Surname string of voter as recorded in poll book | Character | 40 |
| Stdsur | Standardised surname string, retaining first letter but removing subsequent vowels and repeat consonants | Character | 35 |
| Scode | Russell Soundex code of surname string | Character | 5 |
| Fname | Forename string of voter as recorded in poll book | Character | 25 |
| Shtname | Standardised forename string, using first four characters | Character | 4 |
| Parish | Parish of residence coded from poll book | Character | 1 |
| Street | Street of residence simplified from poll book | Character | 40 |
| Occup | Occupation of voter as recorded in poll book | Character | 30 |
| Oclv4 | Revised Booth/Armstrong classification of occupation of the voter as recorded in poll book | Character | 8 |
| Oclv3 | Revised Booth/Armstrong classification of occupational trade cluster of the voter | Character | 7 |
| Oclv2 | Revised Booth/Armstrong classification of occupational sub-sector of the voter | Character | 4 |
| Oclv1 | Revised Booth/Armstrong classification of occupational sector of the voter | Character | 2 |
| Vote | Coded vote entered as recorded in poll book | Character | 6 |
| Lineno | Line number of each entry within a parish in each table | Number | 6 |

Moreover, when a street was known by more than one name this was standardised to what seemed to be the most frequently occurring form. Thus Oxford Street was known not only by that name, but also as 'Oxford Road' and 'Acton Road'; however the common form 'OXFORD ST' was adopted for all of these. Finally variant spellings were standardised. Thus 'Aire Street' and 'Ayre Street' were entered as 'AIR ST'. It is recognised that these procedures involved the application of the historian's judgement, and that the purist would have created look-up tables to accommodate address variants. It will be noted that common contractions such as 'ST' for street, 'LA' for lane, 'CT' for court, 'PASS' for passage, 'RD' for road, 'AY' for alley and 'SQ' for square were employed throughout. Finally, all letters in the database were entered in upper case, which is worth noting as database querying software may be case-sensitive.

The field *Stdsur* contains the standardised surname string, created by running a computer program which examined each letter of the surname string sequentially. If the letter was not a vowel (A,E,I,O,U,Y) and was not the same as the previous letter, then it was retained. If the letter was a vowel (after the first character), or if it was the same as the previous letter, then it was discarded. The effect was to retain the initial letter of the surname string, but to delete the second of pairs of consecutively repeated consonants and to delete vowels found after the first character. The field *Scode* contains the Russell Soundex code for the surname string.[1] Russell Soundex coding retains the initial letter of the surname string, and removes any terminal 'S' from that string. The letters 'W' and 'H' are ignored, as are other characters not mentioned below, such as apostrophes. The letters 'A', 'E', 'I', 'O', 'U' and 'Y' are treated as separators. They are never coded (except internally), and are only output as the initial letter of the surname. When two characters which would receive the same coded value are not separated by a separator a single code is produced.[2] The coding of the remaining letters is given in Table 3.3.

To be included in the Westminster Historical Database, then, individual-level records of voting behaviour had to survive from the period. For these poll book records to exist, it was necessary that there should have been a contested election. Election contests took place when there were more candidates than there were seats available to represent the constituency. In general elections Westminster returned two Members of Parliament, whilst in by-elections just one was returned to fill a vacancy.[3] Contested by-elections occurred in 1749, 1788 and 1818, and in these elections each elector had one vote at his disposal.[4] In all other contested elections two seats were contested, and each elector had two votes at his disposal. However, he was under no obligation to use both votes, and if he did so he was under no obligation to give both votes to political allies.

**Table 3.3 Russell Soundex coding of surname characters**

| Character | Code |
|---|---|
| B,F,P,V | 2 |
| C,G,J,K,Q,S,X,Z | 3 |
| D,T | 4 |
| L | 5 |
| M,N | 6 |
| R | 7 |

Party structures in the late eighteenth and early nineteenth centuries were amorphous and fluid; indeed, not until 1970 were voters in British parliamentary elections told officially for which political party each candidate was standing.[5] The Westminster Historical Database therefore avoids the political labelling of candidates: this ascription is something which is left to the user of the Database. Nevertheless, although general elections were frequently contested by three candidates, some were clearly politically dichotomised (1780 and 1784, for example), whilst others were equally clearly three-cornered contests, such as that of 1818.

Contemporary election returns made no official record of the number of votes gained by each candidate. However, unofficial contemporary sources such as newspapers frequently record the total vote achieved by each candidate. Given the loss of data from the manuscript poll books, the number voting for each candidate in the Database rarely coincides with the number recorded in these unofficial contemporary sources. But comparison of the unofficial returns with the numbers recorded in the Database suggest that the two were broadly consistent. The names of the candidates standing at each of the elections during the period 1749-1820 are tabulated below, together with details of how many votes were gained by each as recorded in the *History of Parliament*.

## Table 3.4 Election contests in Westminster, 1749-1820

| **15 May 1750** | **Votes received** |
|---|---|
| GRANVILLE LEVESON GOWER (Viscount Trentham) | 4,811 |
| Sir George Vandeput | 4,654 |

| **20 April 1754** | |
|---|---|
| EDWARD CORNWALLIS | 3,385 |
| Sir JOHN CROSSE | 3,184 |
| James Edward Oglethorpe | 261 |
| Charles Sackville (Earl of Middlesex) | 209 |

| **26 October 1774** | |
|---|---|
| HUGH PERCY (Lord Percy) | 4,994 |
| Lord THOMAS PELHAM CLINTON | 4,774 |
| Hervey Redmond Morres (Viscount Mountmorres) | 2,531 |
| Charles Stanhope (Viscount Mahon) | 2,342 |
| Humphrey Cotes | 130 |

| **10 October 1780** | |
|---|---|
| Sir GEORGE BRYDGES RODNEY | 5,298 |
| Hon. CHARLES JAMES FOX | 4,878 |
| Lord Thomas Pelham Clinton (Lord Lincoln) | 4,157 |

| **12 May 1784** | |
|---|---|
| Sir SAMUEL HOOD, Bt (Baron Hood) | 6,588 |
| Hon. CHARLES JAMES FOX | 6,126 |
| Sir Cecil Wray | 5,895 |

| **4 August 1788** | |
|---|---|
| Lord JOHN TOWNSHEND | 6,392 |
| Sir Samuel Hood, Bt (Baron Hood) | 5,569 |

| **2 July 1790** | |
|---|---|
| Hon. CHARLES JAMES FOX | 3,516 |
| Sir SAMUEL HOOD, Bt (Baron Hood) | 3,217 |
| John Horne Tooke | 1,697 |

| **13 June 1796** | |
|---|---|
| Hon. CHARLES JAMES FOX | 5,160 |

| | |
|---|---|
| Sir ALAN GARDNER, Bt | 4,814 |
| John Horne Tooke | 2,819 |

**15 July 1802**

| | |
|---|---|
| Hon. CHARLES JAMES FOX | 2,671 |
| Sir ALAN GARDNER, Bt (Baron Gardner) | 2,431 |
| John Graham | 1,693 |

**19 November 1806**

| | |
|---|---|
| Sir SAMUEL HOOD | 5,478 |
| RICHARD BRINSLEY SHERIDAN | 4,758 |
| James Paull | 4,481 |

**23 May 1807**

| | |
|---|---|
| Sir FRANCIS BURDETT, Bt | 5,134 |
| THOMAS COCHRANE (Lord Cochrane) | 3,708 |
| Richard Brinsley Sheridan | 2,645 |
| John Elliott | 2,137 |
| James Paull | 269 |

**4 July 1818**

| | |
|---|---|
| Sir SAMUEL ROMILLY | 5,339 |
| Sir FRANCIS BURDETT, Bt | 5,238 |
| Sir Murray Maxwell | 4,808 |
| Henry Hunt | 84 |
| Hon. Douglas James William Kinnaird | 65 |
| John Cartwright | 23 |

**3 March 1819**

| | |
|---|---|
| Hon. GEORGE LAMB | 4,465 |
| John Cam Hobhouse | 3,861 |
| John Cartwright | 38 |

**25 July 1820**

| | |
|---|---|
| Sir FRANCIS BURDETT, Bt | 5,327 |
| JOHN CAM HOBHOUSE | 4,882 |
| Hon. George Lamb | 4,436 |

Notes: Members of Parliament are shown in capitals. The voting figures for the election of 1749, where the date given is of the return, record the number of votes given to each candidate. The scrutiny reduced these figures to Leveson Gower, 4,103 and Vandeput, 3,933. Sir Samuel Hood, Bt (elected 1784; defeated 1788; elected 1790) was cousin to Sir Samuel Hood (elected 1806). No individual-level data survive for the contested elections of 1754 and 1807.

Source: R. Sedgwick (ed.), *The House of Commons, 1715-54* (2 vols, 1970), i, p. 285; L.B. Namier and J. Brooke (eds), *The House of Commons, 1754-90* (3 vols, 1964), i, pp. 335-6; R.G. Thorne (ed.), *The House of Commons, 1790-1820* (5 vols, 1986), ii, pp. 266-7; Anon., *Tables, shewing the progressive state of the poll* (1820).

It was not just the frequency of contested elections (twelve in 46 years) that made Westminster an atypical constituency. Doubts were expressed in 1762 whether the son of Lord Sandys was of sufficient 'quality' to represent the constituency which lay in the shadow of the court and the seat of government, and where many of the country's leading nobility and gentry lived for at least part of the year. Few of the candidates in these elections, and fewer still of the constituency's representatives, were not born to the purple. Irish peers stood against the sons of English peers, and when the government interest was represented by the Senior Service, scarcely less than an admiral would do. Suggestions in the early nineteenth century that the great trading constituency should be represented by a 'commercial man' had little effect,[6] and only when the tradesmen of the Westminster Committee put forward the name of a wealthy baronet to be their representative did they achieve success.[7]

Westminster experienced a by-election in 1749 that long remained in the public memory. Trentham's[8] appointment to office in that year led to a vigorous challenge from Vandeput,[9] the candidate of the Independent Electors of Westminster. But between then and 1770 a political hiatus ensued as successive governments sought to avoid election contests in Westminster by selecting uncontroversial candidates (the contest of 1754 was not serious, and will not be mentioned again). The strategy was successful, but metropolitan Wilkite radicalism infected the constituency in the late 1760s, and in 1770 Sir Robert Bernard was elected unopposed. He was the first opponent of the government to be elected since 1741, but he was not the harbinger of a new radical tradition. In 1774 the Wilkite candidates, Mountmorres[10] and Mahon,[11] were easily defeated by Percy[12] and Pelham Clinton (Lord Lincoln).[13]

**Table 3.5 *Vote* codes and distribution of votes in Table P1749**

| Code | Political choice | Number of Records |
|------|------------------|-------------------|
| 01 | Vandeput | 4,654 |
| 10 | Trentham | 4,809 |
| **Total** | | **9,463** |

**Table 3.6 *Vote* codes and distribution of votes in Table P1774**

| Code | Political choice | Number of Records |
|-------|------------------|-------------------|
| 00001 | Cotes | 35 |
| 00010 | Mahon | 13 |
| 00011 | Mahon and Cotes | 14 |
| 00100 | Mountmorres | 31 |
| 00101 | Mountmorres and Cotes | 35 |
| 00110 | Mountmorres and Mahon | 2,257 |
| 01000 | Clinton | 59 |
| 01001 | Clinton and Cotes | 15 |
| 01010 | Clinton and Mahon | 20 |
| 01100 | Clinton and Mountmorres | 35 |
| 10000 | Percy | 160 |
| 10001 | Percy and Cotes | 26 |
| 10010 | Percy and Mahon | 19 |
| 10100 | Percy and Mountmorres | 175 |
| 11000 | Percy and Clinton | 4,620 |
| **Total** | | **7,514** |

The recrudescence of metropolitan radicalism owed much to the American war, which led to petitioning movements throughout the country. Yorkshire's lead in petitioning was soon taken up in Westminster.[14] In February 1780 Charles James Fox[15] became chairman of the Westminster Committee of Association, and was adopted as a candidate for the constituency.[16] But the Whig myth was more sustaining than evanescent Wilkite agitations, and the cause persisted through the years. In 1780 the Administration misjudged Fox's appeal to the voters, and he was elected in second

place on the poll to Admiral Rodney.[17] 'It was a mistake to propose Lord Lincoln' declared Edward Gibbon to Lord Sheffield, 'he
is disliked by the substantial tradesmen: but they abhor Fox'.[18] The
Westminster Database is ideally suited to testing this *obiter dictum*
from eighteenth-century England's greatest historian. Lord Lincoln
was defeated, despite the Treasury expenditure of over £8,000 in
the constituency.

**Table 3.7 *Vote* codes and distribution of votes in Table P1780**

| Code | Political choice | Number of Records |
|------|------------------|-------------------|
| **001** | Lincoln | 588 |
| **010** | Rodney | 129 |
| **011** | Rodney and Lincoln | 3,551 |
| **100** | Fox | 3,128 |
| **101** | Fox and Lincoln | 119 |
| **110** | Fox and Rodney | 1,619 |
| **Total** | | **9,134** |

Fox's claim to be the 'man of the people' and the champion of
reform was subsequently tarnished after his coalition with Lord
North in 1782 and the promotion of the East India Bill.[19] Wray,
who had been elected unopposed in a by-election in 1782,[20] was
denounced as a turncoat and pilloried as 'Judas' in the Foxite press
when he stood with Hood[21] against Fox in 1784.[22] The Treasury
spent lavishly in an attempt to keep Fox out of Westminster; and
having failed it sought to use the scrutiny to prevent him taking his
seat.[23]

Hood's appointment to office in 1788 led to a by-election in
which he was defeated by Fox's colleague Townshend.[24] But the
cost to both sides in the elections of 1784 and 1788 forced a compromise upon them. In 1790 it was agreed that henceforth each
side should put up one candidate only in the ensuing elections.

The agreement of 1790 was honoured, but it provoked an un-
foreseen response from Horne Tooke, the erstwhile Wilkite who
had supported Pitt and Hood in 1788.[25] Horne Tooke opposed this
attempt to deprive the electors of Westminster of their political
voices. Standing in 1790, without an adequate organisation, he was
roundly beaten.

**Table 3.8** *Vote* **codes and distribution of votes in Table P1784**

| Code | Political choice | Number of Records |
|------|------------------|-------------------|
| 001 | Fox | 4,872 |
| 010 | Wray | 259 |
| 011 | Wray and Fox | 67 |
| 100 | Hood | 122 |
| 101 | Hood and Fox | 841 |
| 110 | Hood and Wray | 5,266 |
| **Total** | | **11,427** |

**Table 3.9** *Vote* **codes and distribution of votes in Table P1788**

| Code | Political choice | Number of Records |
|------|------------------|-------------------|
| 01 | Townshend | 4,279 |
| 10 | Hood | 3,947 |
| **Total** | | **8,226** |

**Table 3.10** *Vote* **codes and distribution of votes in Table P1790**

| Code | Political choice | Number of Records |
|------|------------------|-------------------|
| 001 | Horne Tooke | 671 |
| 010 | Hood | 1,155 |
| 011 | Hood and Horne Tooke | 501 |
| 100 | Fox | 1,708 |
| 101 | Fox and Horne Tooke | 136 |
| 110 | Fox and Hood | 844 |
| **Total** | | **5,015** |

Horne Tooke stood again in 1796, this time with the support of some of the London Corresponding Society. Again he was defeated, although by a narrower margin. Whilst Fox and Gardner[26] had a covert alliance in 1796, Horne Tooke directed his fire towards the latter, and he appealed to his supporters to give their second votes to Fox.

**Table 3.11** *Vote* **codes and distribution of votes in Table P1796**

| Code | Political choice | Number of Records |
|------|------------------|-------------------|
| 001 | Horne Tooke | 464 |
| 010 | Gardner | 597 |
| 011 | Gardner and Horne Tooke | 3 |
| 100 | Fox | 571 |
| 101 | Fox and Horne Tooke | 1,078 |
| 110 | Fox and Gardner | 345 |
| **Total** | | **3,058** |

By 1802 Horne Tooke had left the most democratic constituency in the country to pursue his campaign for parliamentary reform and freedom of election in the improbable constituency of Old Sarum. John Graham stood for Westminster, urging that so important a commercial centre should be represented by a businessman, and appealing to the electors in 'the middle ranks of society'.[27] Graham fared no better than Horne Tooke. The election ended after nine days, when it was clear that he had no hope of winning, and he returned to obscurity.

**Table 3.12** *Vote* **codes and distribution of votes in Table P1802**

| Code | Political choice | Number of Records |
|------|------------------|-------------------|
| 001 | Graham | 1,089 |
| 010 | Gardner | 903 |
| 011 | Gardner and Graham | 21 |
| 100 | Fox | 552 |
| 101 | Fox and Graham | 589 |
| 110 | Fox and Gardner | 1,528 |
| **Total** | | **4,682** |

Fox's death in 1806 led to a by-election in which Percy was elected unopposed with support from both the Foxite Whigs and the Administration. But the government could not long survive the death of Fox, and its fall led to another general election. Anxious to assume the Foxite mantle in Westminster, Sheridan[28] announced his candidature in the general election of 1806. He stood on a joint ticket with Hood,[29] the government candidate, and appealed for votes to be split between the two, although worries about the sharing of election expenses precluded a formal joint campaign and joint committee. They were opposed by James Paull, who had the support of Burdett, Cartwright, and former members of the London Corresponding Society.[30] Sheridan was elected with Hood, but his majority of only 300 over Paull was humiliating.

Paull stood again in 1807, but quarrelled with Burdett and duelled with him.[31] Burdett declined to risk any more of his fortune in politics, having already spent a great deal in the Middlesex campaigns, but he agreed to represent Westminster if elected without effort on his part. The Westminster Committee thereupon dumped Paull and organised subscriptions to fund a popular election. By parsimony, voluntary labour, and the eschewing of traditional campaigning methods, the Committee managed Burdett's election with an expenditure of only £780.[32] The Portland ministry backed John Elliott, a Westminster brewer, whilst Cochrane[33] claimed to be free of all ties. Burdett and Cochrane were elected after the attempts by Sheridan and Cochrane to make truces with the Westminster Committee were rebuffed.

**Table 3.13** *Vote* **codes and distribution of votes in Table P1806**

| Code | Political choice | Number of Records |
|------|------------------|-------------------|
| 001  | Paull            | 1,495             |
| 010  | Hood             | 481               |
| 011  | Hood and Paull   | 526               |
| 100  | Sheridan         | 459               |
| 101  | Sheridan and Hood | 178              |
| 110  | Sheridan and Paull | 1,472           |
| **Total** |             | **4,611**         |

Six candidates stood in the election of 1818: on Burdett's radical flank stood Hunt,[34] Kinnaird[35] and Cartwright,[36] whilst Sir Samuel Romilly's[37] mainstream Whig candidature and that of Sir Murray Maxwell[38] in the Administration interest put pressure on Burdett's opposite flank. Afraid of Burdett's losing altogether, Francis Place's Westminster Committee jettisoned Kinnaird during the election, finding Romilly to be an acceptable candidate when it became clear that they could not defeat both him and Maxwell. In the event, Burdett was elected in second place to Romilly, with Maxwell not far behind. The pretensions of Kinnaird, Hunt and Cartwright were shown to be of little significance.

**Table 3.14 *Vote* codes and distribution of votes in Table P1818**

| Code | Political choice | Number of Records |
|------|------------------|-------------------|
| 000001 | Hunt | 15 |
| 000010 | Cartwright | 4 |
| 000011 | Cartwright and Hunt | 3 |
| 000100 | Maxwell | 2,150 |
| 000101 | Maxwell and Hunt | 0 |
| 000110 | Maxwell and Cartwright | 4 |
| 001000 | Romilly | 426 |
| 001001 | Romilly and Hunt | 1 |
| 001010 | Romilly and Cartwright | 0 |
| 001100 | Romilly and Maxwell | 2,318 |
| 010000 | Kinnaird | 6 |
| 010001 | Kinnaird and Hunt | 0 |
| 010010 | Kinnaird and Cartwright | 0 |
| 010100 | Kinnaird and Maxwell | 8 |
| 011000 | Kinnaird and Romilly | 10 |
| 100000 | Burdett | 2,312 |
| 100001 | Burdett and Hunt | 40 |
| 100010 | Burdett and Cartwright | 12 |
| 100100 | Burdett and Maxwell | 265 |
| 101000 | Burdett and Romilly | 2,490 |
| 110000 | Burdett and Kinnaird | 74 |
| **Total** | | **10,138** |

What might thereafter have become a stable compromise between the moderation of Burdett and Romilly against the still-powerful forces opposed to reform was shattered by Romilly's suicide in 1818. Kinnaird's name was widely canvassed to assume Romilly's seat, but the reformers had to avoid offending the Whigs, to whom Kinnaird was unacceptable. Hobhouse[39] was an acceptable candidate to both Whigs and moderate reformers, although the suggestion of collusion between the two groups inspired Cartwright to stand again. But the desire of the reform group to assert its independence from the Whigs offended the latter, who nominated George Lamb.[40] Little distinguished the moderation of Hobhouse from that of Lamb, although the two gentlemen-reformers pitched their appeals to different elements of the electorate. The shock to the reformers of Romilly's success in 1818 was small compared with that of 1819, which saw Lamb elected with a majority of over 600 votes over Hobhouse.[41]

The death of George III in 1820 brought the parliament to an end, and the general election of that year, contested by Burdett, Hobhouse and Lamb, saw the defeat of Lamb. Thereafter Hobhouse sat for Westminster until 1832, and Burdett until 1837. But the glory was departed. Neither was a radical in the manner of Hunt or Cartwright, and their moderate Independence had a broad appeal in the prosperous commercial constituency.

**Table 3.15 *Vote* codes and distribution of votes in Table P1819**

| Code | Political choice | Number of Records |
|------|------------------|-------------------|
| 001 | Lamb | 3,493 |
| 010 | Cartwright | 21 |
| 100 | Hobhouse | 3,042 |
| **Total** | | **6,556** |

**Table 3.16 *Vote* codes and distribution of votes in Table P1820**

| Code | Political choice | Number of Records |
|------|------------------|-------------------|
| 001 | Hobhouse | 106 |
| 010 | Lamb | 3,016 |
| 011 | Lamb and Hobhouse | 48 |
| 100 | Burdett | 23 |
| 101 | Burdett and Hobhouse | 3,884 |
| 110 | Burdett and Lamb | 509 |
| **Total** | | **7,586** |

Westminster was divided into nine parishes. Whilst polling took place centrally at the hustings erected in the open area in front of St Paul's church in Covent Garden, the hustings were divided into seven booths and voters polled at the appropriate booth for their parish of residence.[42] Manuscript poll books thus correspond to these polling booths for parishes or grouped parishes: voters from St Margaret and St John polled together, as did those from St Clement and St Mary. For this reason they have been referred to throughout in this combined form. Voters from the Liberty of St Martin-le-Grand generally polled at the booth for St Paul, although in 1819 and 1820 they polled with those from St Anne as well as St Paul. However, in tables **P1819** and **P1820** the data for St Anne and St Paul with St Martin-le-Grand have been disaggregated during data entry. The other parishes had their own polling booths: these were for St George, St Martin, St James, and (except for 1819 and 1820 noted above) St Anne. But voters were so numerous that even this division could not accommodate them within one manuscript poll book.[43] Sometimes two poll books were in use simultaneously in one polling booth, as for St Margaret and St John in 1788. At other times poll books were used consecutively, as in the same parishes in 1819.[44] Each parish has been allocated a code:

**Table 3.17** *Parish* **codes in poll book tables**

| Code | Parish |
|------|--------|
| A | St Anne, Soho |
| B | St Clement Danes, and St Mary-le-Strand |
| C | St George, Hanover Square |
| D | St James, Piccadilly |
| E | St Margaret, Westminster, and St John the Evangelist |
| F | St Martin-in-the-Fields |
| G | St Paul, Covent Garden, and St Martin-le-Grand |

One of the greatest challenges confronting users of the Westminster Historical Database stems from loss of data. Of itself, this is a familiar problem for historians. And yet political historians whose use of poll books has been confined to printed editions may not appreciate the magnitude of the problems with manuscript versions. For example, complete data exist for St Anne's parish in 1784, but only about half the records survive for that parish four years later. It is thus possible to state with confidence that an individual polling in 1784 was the only person of that name in St Anne to have voted in 1784. And yet if only one individual of that name were recorded four years later, there would be no certainty that he was the same person as the one who polled previously. Random data survival is the opposite side of a coin which bears random data loss on the other face. In cases of missing data we do not know whether individuals are linked because they were genuinely mobile in terms of occupation and residence, or because of the contingency of data survival.

**Table 3.18 Records by *Parish* in poll book tables**

|  | A | B | C | D | E | F | G | Total |
|---|---|---|---|---|---|---|---|---|
| **P1749** | 707 | 885 | 1,463 | 2,112 | 1,865 | 1,962 | 469 | **9,463** |
| **P1774** | 610 | 971 | 1,265 | 1,587 | 1,137 | 1,540 | 404 | **7,514** |
| **P1780** | 681 | 1,131 | 1,614 | 1,773 | 1,723 | 1,772 | 440 | **9,134** |
| **P1784** | 908 | 1,464 | 2,325 | 1,586 | 2,337 | 2,265 | 542 | **11,427** |
| **P1788** | 637 | 498 | 2,182 | 407 | 2,061 | 1,889 | 552 | **8,226** |
| **P1790** | 528 | 752 | 1,133 | 648 | 679 | 1,275 | 0 | **5,015** |
| **P1796** | 367 | 0 | 0 | 284 | 1,241 | 888 | 278 | **3,058** |
| **P1802** | 386 | 625 | 766 | 877 | 701 | 1,015 | 312 | **4,682** |
| **P1806** | 911 | 1,113 | 20 | 1,086 | 1,036 | 445 | 0 | **4,611** |
| **P1818** | 901 | 1,219 | 2,211 | 2,060 | 1,554 | 1,746 | 447 | **10,138** |
| **P1819** | 489 | 963 | 1,334 | 1,056 | 1,045 | 1,510 | 159 | **6,556** |
| **P1820** | 806 | 1,182 | 1,213 | 1,751 | 1,477 | 761 | 396 | **7,586** |
| **Total** | **7,931** | **10,803** | **15,526** | **15,227** | **16,856** | **17,068** | **3,999** | **87,410** |

A number of poll books have been damaged, principally by water. Sometimes the poll books for entire parishes have not survived, whilst for other parishes they are only available in parts. All available manuscript poll books for the years 1784, 1788, 1790, 1796, 1802, 1806, 1819 and 1820 have been entered into the Westminster Historical Database. For the election of 1784 the poll books were virtually complete and available on microfilm, whilst the poll books for 1802 were entire. The major *lacunae* were to be found in the elections of 1790 and 1796. Details have survived of the voting behaviour of only about 5,000 voters in 1790, and for about 3,000 in the election six years later. In this latter case the original poll books were supplemented by two contemporary transcripts. One for St Margaret and St John, apparently complete, has been incorporated into the Database.[45] Another lists plumpers (single votes) for Fox, plumpers for Horne Tooke, and split votes for Fox and Horne Tooke, from St Anne, St Martin, and St Paul with St Martin-le-Grand.[46] The original poll book of St George in 1788 was replaced by a contemporary transcript, doubtless once the property of an election agent.[47] But no attempt was made to supplement fragments of the voting record of any one parish with fragments from another source: thus the incomplete record of St James in 1784 was not supplemented with the incomplete and partially illegible transcript in the Guildhall Library.[48] The transcript of the poll book of the 1784 election in the Huntington Library has not been consulted.[49]

It will be seen from Table 3.18 that the poll book records of some parishes have experienced a better survival rate than those of others. Only St Paul has suffered the complete loss of data for two elections; but this is in part a function of the small size of the parish. Since St Paul's voters were easily accommodated within a single poll book, loss of a single book entailed loss of all data for the parish. But for other parishes, most notably St George, St James and St Martin, the loss of a single poll book had a limited impact on missing data. However, the cumulative effect of missing data for these parishes is nonetheless considerable.

**Table 3.19 Sources of poll book data**

**1749**  Anon., *A copy of the poll for a citizen for the City and Liberty of Westminster* (1749).

**1774**  Anon., *A correct copy of the poll, for electing two representatives in parliament, for the City and Liberty of Westminster* (1774).

**1780 LMA**  Westminster poll books (1780): St Margaret and St John, WR/PP/1780/1-3; St Anne, WR/PP/1780/4-5; Anon., *Copy of the poll for the election of two citizens to serve in the present parliament for the City and Liberty of Westminster* (1780).

**1784 LMA**  Westminster poll books (1784): St Anne, WR/PP/1784/1-2; St Clement and St Mary, WR/PP/1784/3-5; St George, WR/PP/1784/6-10; St James, WR/PP/1784/11, 13-15; St Margaret and St John, WR/PP/1784/16-20; St Martin, WR/PP/1784/21-5; St Paul and St Martin-le-Grand, WR/PP/1784/26-7.

**1788** LMA Westminster poll books (1788): St Margaret and St John, WR/PP/1788/1-3; St Paul and St Martin-le-Grand, WR/PP/1788/4; St Anne, WR/PP/1788/5; St James, WR/PP/1788/8; St Martin, WR/PP/1788/15-18; St Clement and St Mary, WR/PP/1788/20-1; St George, WR/PP/1788/23.

**1790** LMA Westminster poll books (1790): St Margaret and St John, WR/PP/1790/1; St Anne, WR/PP/1790/4; St James, WR/PP/1790/5, 7; St George, WR/PP/1790/8-9; St Martin, WR/PP/1790/10-11; St Clement and St Mary, WR/PP/1790/12-13.

**1796** LMA Westminster poll books (1796): St James, WR/PP/1796/3. Guildhall MS poll for Westminster (1796): St Anne, St Martin, St Paul and St Martin-le-Grand. WAC Westminster poll books (1796): St Margaret and St John, E/3081A.

**1802** LMA Westminster poll books (1802): St Margaret and St John, WR/PP/1802/1-2; St Paul and St Martin-le-Grand, WR/PP/1802/3; St Anne, WR/PP/1802/4; St James, WR/PP/1802/5-6; St George, WR/PP/1802/7-8; St Martin, WR/PP/1802/9-10; St Clement and St Mary, WR/PP/1802/11.

**1806** LMA Westminster poll books (1806): St Margaret and St John, WR/PP/1806/1, 3-5; St Anne, WR/PP/1806/9-10; St James, WR/PP/1806/11-13, 15; St George, WR/PP/1806/21; St Martin, WR/PP/1806/22; St Clement and St Mary, WR/PP/1806/27-9.

**1818** Anon., *The poll book, for electing two representatives in parliament for the City and Liberty of Westminster* (1818).

**1819** LMA Westminster poll books (1819): St Margaret and St John, WR/PP/1819/1-8; St Anne, St Paul and St Martin-le-Grand WR/PP/1819/11-15; St James, WR/PP/1819/16-19; St George, WR/PP/1819/25-32; St Martin, WR/PP/1819/33-42; St Clement and St Mary, WR/PP/1819/43-8.

**1820** LMA Westminster poll books (1820): St Margaret and St John, WR/PP/1820/1-8; St Anne, St Paul and St Martin-le-Grand, WR/PP/1820/9-14; St James, WR/PP/1820/15-21; St George, WR/PP/1820/22-3, 26-9; St Martin, WR/PP/1820/31-3; St Clement and St Mary, WR/PP/1820/35-41.

## 3.2 Rate books

Rate book tables exist only for selected years within the period. Only selected rate books have been entered into the Database tables. The guiding principle of selection was that they should provide data to supplement the poll books. So rate book data were only collected for years with a contested election, and then only for parishes for which poll books survived. Rate book data were also collected for two parishes thought to have contrasting social and economic characteristics. St Margaret and St John, in the west of the constituency, was seen as being a 'Court' parish, the centre of government, and an area into which the new buildings of Westminster were spreading.[50] By contrast St Anne, in the north-east of the constituency, was dominated to an even greater degree than the constituency as a whole by artisans and craftsmen. Finally, rate book data were collected for all parishes in two years towards the middle and the end of the period. An abundance of poll book data available for potential linkage from the elections of 1784 and 1818 led to these years being selected for more detailed study. Whilst voters for the Liberty of the Savoy polled at the booth for the parishes of St Clement and St Mary, it would appear that, through oversight, no rate book data were collected for the Liberty in these years; however, the number of cases overlooked is likely to have been small.

Table 3.32 shows the rate book data collected by year and parish. The count of the number of records in the Database was taken after the data validation operation outlined below, that is, after eliminating corporate bodies and households rated in a woman's name. It is thus substantially less than the numbers of rated properties, but for 1784 and 1818 it represents a rough estimate of the number of householders eligible to vote.[51]

The elections of 1788 and 1790 were so close together that data from the rate books for 1789 for St Anne and St Margaret and St John were entered. Similarly, data were entered from the rate books of 1818 on the assumption that they could be used to illuminate voting behaviour not only in that year but also in 1819 and 1820. The rates for St Margaret and St John were for an 'omnibus' rate for the relief of the poor, the maintenance of the highways, and the provision of a scavenger. Thus they do not suffer from the problems of comparability of rates discussed earlier in Chapter 2 and noted by Elizabeth Baigent in her study of Bristol rate assessments.

**Table 3.20 Rate book tables in the Westminster Historical Database**

| Table Name | Description | Number of Records |
|---|---|---|
| R1749 | Rate book data, 1749 | 1,145 |
| R1774 | Rate book data, 1774 | 3,900 |
| R1780 | Rate book data, 1780 | 3,828 |
| R1784 | Rate book data, 1784 | 15,748 |
| R1789 | Rate book data, 1789 | 4,174 |
| R1796 | Rate book data, 1796 | 2,864 |
| R1802 | Rate book data, 1802 | 3,493 |
| R1806 | Rate book data, 1806 | 3,641 |
| R1818 | Rate book data, 1818-19 | 17,637 |
| **Total** | | **56,430** |

Many of the fields found in the poll book tables are replicated in the rate book tables, where they are treated in the same way. The fields *Surname*, *Stdsur*, *Scode*, *Fname*, *Shtname*, *Parish* and *Street* are common to both poll book and rate book tables. Thus users who wish to see how street names in rate book tables were standardised should consult section 3.1 above. But in addition to those which may be used for record linkage purposes, rate book tables also contain the fields *Ward* and *Rv*, as well as a line number (*Lineno*) which in conjunction with *Parish* uniquely identifies each record within a table.

The field *Ward* indicates a subdivision of a parish, and exists in the original rate book as a rate collector's 'round'. Most parishes were divided into two or more wards, the exceptions being St Paul, St Mary and St John. However, since at each election voters in St Mary polled with those of St Clement, St Mary may be considered as a ward of St Clement and St Mary. Similarly, at each election voters from St John polled with those of St Margaret, so St John may be considered as a ward of St Margaret and St John. Only in St Paul, then, are linked poll and rate book tables incapable of being further subdivided to facilitate finer spatial analysis. Data pertaining to wards were entered after data entry by allocating to each ward records between specified line numbers within a parish.

Unfortunately, the sorting of rate data for St Margaret and St John in 1802 means that ward data are unavailable for that parish in that year.

The field *Rv* contains the crucial additional data supplied by the rate books, namely the interval data of the rack rental valuations of real estate in Westminster. And yet these rack rental valuations are not without their problems. In the first place, there is no certainty that the rack rental assessments recorded represent the true rental value of the householder's property. Frequently the rate assessments in St Margaret and St John were based upon a valuation of three quarters of the rack rent, and in these cases it is the reduced valuation which has been taken. The rateable value should thus be taken as no more than a valuation relative to other rated properties in the parish in any one year. There is no reason to suppose that the basis of valuation was entirely consistent between parishes in any one year, nor within a parish between years.

Fields which were common to both poll and rate book tables were standardised consistently, as outlined above. Line numbers (*Lineno*) were entered sequentially during data entry, and together with information on the *Parish* and the table they uniquely identify each record.

But the rate books contained supplementary information relating to statuses, which has been omitted from the Database. Status designations in the name field of the rate books were removed for consistency. These included the following: 'Mr', 'Mrs', 'Widow', 'Miss', 'Reverend', 'Dr', 'Sir', 'Lord', 'Duke of', 'Earl', 'Viscount', 'Bishop of', 'Prince of', 'Countess of', 'Lady', 'Admiral', 'Colonel', 'Major', 'General' and 'Captain'.

Business partnerships found in the rate books were identified by the ampersand, and the rack rent split equally between the partners. Any remainder was attributed to the first-named partner. Thus 'Mayhew & Ince £15' was entered as 'Mayhew £8' and 'Ince £7'. In the case of 'Smith & Co.' the entire rack rent was attributed to Smith. These business partnerships are identified by the letter D in the field *Comp*, and by having consecutive line numbers within the parish.

The rate book files were searched prior to being imported into the Database and entries for identifiable females such as 'Mary Smith' were omitted. Also omitted were empty properties, unrated properties such as 'Parish Workhouse' or 'Charity School', and other corporate bodies which had not been identified in the search for the ampersand, such as 'Market House', 'Pantheon Proprietors', 'Admiralty' and 'Waterworks Commissioners'. Partnerships of two or more women were entirely eliminated under this procedure, whilst those of a man and a woman, such as 'John Smith & Mary Evans £24' had their rack rent attributed entirely to the male partner.

**Table 3.21 Standard format for rate book tables**

| Field Name | Description | Data Type | Field Length |
|---|---|---|---|
| **Surname** | Surname string of voter as recorded in rate book | Character | 40 |
| **Stdsur** | Standardised surname string, retaining first letter but removing subsequent vowels and repeat consonants | Character | 35 |
| **Scode** | Russell Soundex code of surname string | Character | 5 |
| **Fname** | Forename string of voter as recorded in rate book | Character | 25 |
| **Shtname** | Standardised forename string, using first four characters | Character | 4 |
| **Parish** | Parish of residence coded from rate book | Character | 1 |
| **Street** | Street of residence simplified from rate book | Character | 40 |
| **Ward** | Ward of residence coded from rate book | Character | 1 |
| **Rv** | Rack rental value of property taken from rate book | Number | 3 |
| **Comp** | Indicator of a company or business partnership | Character | 1 |
| **Lineno** | Line number of each entry within a parish in each table | Number | 6 |

As was described above, the rate book data were intended to supplement the core poll book database rather than to stand alone. The elimination of cases outlined here shows that rate book tables should not be used to analyse the distribution of real estate within Westminster or any purpose which seeks to translate the data directly to a reality 'on the ground'. Proximity in the rate book tables (indicated by consecutive line numbers within a ward) does not imply physical propinquity within the urban environment, and might be caused by no more than the elimination of intervening cases. Still more clearly, it cannot be used to examine the role of women within Westminster, since cases relating to identifiable women have been eliminated.

**Table 3.22 *Parish* codes in rate book tables**

| Code | Parish |
|------|--------|
| A | St Anne, Soho |
| B | St Clement Danes, and St Mary-le-Strand |
| C | St George, Hanover Square |
| D | St James, Piccadilly |
| E | St Margaret, Westminster, and St John the Evangelist |
| F | St Martin-in-the-Fields |
| G | St Paul, Covent Garden, and St Martin-le-Grand |

**Table 3.23 *Ward* codes in Table R1749**

| Ward code | Parish code | Ward name | Number of Records |
|-----------|-------------|-----------|-------------------|
| A | A | King Square | 664 |
| B | A | Leicester Fields | 481 |
| **Total** | | | **1,145** |

**Table 3.24 *Ward* codes in Table R1774**

| Ward code | Parish code | Ward name | Number of Records |
|-----------|-------------|-----------|-------------------|
| A | A | King Square | 669 |
| B | A | Leicester Fields | 502 |
| C | E | Grand | 813 |
| D | E | Absey | 892 |
| E | E | St John | 1,024 |
| **Total** | | | **3,900** |

## Table 3.25 *Ward* codes in Table R1780

| Ward code | Parish code | Ward name | Number of Records |
|---|---|---|---|
| A | A | King Square | 692 |
| B | A | Leicester Fields | 474 |
| C | E | Grand | 801 |
| D | E | Absey | 882 |
| E | E | St John | 979 |
| Total | | | **3,828** |

## Table 3.26 *Ward* codes in Table R1784

| Ward code | Parish code | Ward name | Number of Records |
|---|---|---|---|
| A | A | King Square | 639 |
| B | A | Leicester Fields | 608 |
| C | B | Royal | 176 |
| D | B | Savoy | 106 |
| E | B | Middle | 205 |
| F | B | Church | 59 |
| G | B | Holywell | 438 |
| H | B | Drury Lane | 253 |
| I | B | Shire Lane | 273 |
| J | B | Temple Bar | 195 |
| K | B | St Mary | 179 |
| L | C | Dover Street | 282 |
| M | C | Conduit Street | 490 |
| N | C | Out | 934 |
| O | C | Grosvenor Street | 743 |
| P | C | Brook Street | 793 |
| Q | D | Pall Mall | 700 |
| R | D | Church | 881 |
| S | D | Golden Square | 866 |
| T | D | Great Marlborough Street | 908 |
| U | E | Grand | 784 |
| V | E | Absey | 907 |
| W | E | St John | 984 |
| X | F | Suffolk Street | 282 |
| Y | F | New Street | 342 |

| Ward code | Parish code | Ward name | Number of Records |
|-----------|-------------|-----------|-------------------|
| Z | F | Charing Cross | 491 |
| 1 | F | Spur Alley | 266 |
| 2 | F | Bedfordbury | 380 |
| 3 | F | Exchange | 317 |
| 4 | F | Strand | 271 |
| 5 | F | Long Acre | 470 |
| 6 | G | St Paul | 526 |
| **Total** | | | **15,748** |

**Table 3.27 *Ward* codes in Table R1789**

| Ward code | Parish code | Ward name | Number of Records |
|-----------|-------------|-----------|-------------------|
| A | A | King Square | 663 |
| B | A | Leicester Fields | 644 |
| C | E | Grand | 827 |
| D | E | Absey | 1,017 |
| E | E | St John | 1,023 |
| **Total** | | | **4,174** |

**Table 3.28 *Ward* codes in Table R1796**

| Ward code | Parish code | Ward name | Number of Records |
|-----------|-------------|-----------|-------------------|
| C | E | Grand | 869 |
| D | E | Absey | 1,010 |
| E | E | St John | 985 |
| **Total** | | | **2,864** |

**Table 3.29 *Ward* codes in Table R1802**

| Ward code | Parish code | Ward name | Number of Records |
|-----------|-------------|-----------|-------------------|
| A | A | King Square | 659 |
| B | A | Leicester Fields | 650 |
| Z | E | St Margaret and St John | 2,184 |
| **Total** | | | **3,493** |

## Table 3.30 *Ward* codes in Table R1806

| Ward code | Parish code | Ward name | Number of Records |
|-----------|-------------|-----------|-------------------|
| A | A | King Square | 658 |
| B | A | Leicester Fields | 675 |
| C | E | Grand | 743 |
| D | E | Absey | 662 |
| E | E | St John | 903 |
| **Total** | | | **3,641** |

## Table 3.31 *Ward* codes in Table R1818

| Ward code | Parish code | Ward name | Number of Records |
|-----------|-------------|-----------|-------------------|
| A | A | King Square | 664 |
| B | A | Leicester Fields | 677 |
| C | B | Royal | 127 |
| D | B | Savoy | 107 |
| E | B | Middle | 188 |
| F | B | Church | 60 |
| G | B | Holywell | 437 |
| H | B | Drury Lane | 260 |
| I | B | Shire Lane | 337 |
| J | B | Temple Bar | 240 |
| K | B | St Mary | 241 |
| L | C | Dover Street | 345 |
| M | C | Conduit Street | 580 |
| N | C | Out | 1,023 |
| O | C | Grosvenor Street | 769 |
| P | C | Brook Street | 902 |
| Q | C | Curzon Street | 725 |
| R | D | Pall Mall | 885 |
| S | D | Church | 915 |
| T | D | Golden Square | 761 |
| U | D | Great Marlborough Street | 1,088 |
| V | E | Grand | 575 |
| W | E | Absey | 1,046 |
| X | E | St John | 1,251 |
| Y | F | Suffolk Street | 298 |

| Ward code | Parish code | Ward name | Number of Records |
|-----------|-------------|-----------|-------------------|
| Z | F | Charing Cross | 472 |
| 1 | F | Spur Alley | 311 |
| 2 | F | Exchange | 271 |
| 3 | F | Strand | 324 |
| 4 | F | New Street | 330 |
| 5 | F | Bedfordbury | 394 |
| 6 | F | Long Acre | 427 |
| 7 | G | St Paul | 607 |
| **Total** | | | **17,637** |

**Table 3.32 Records by *Parish* in rate book tables**

|  | A | B | C | D | E | F | G | Total |
|--|---|---|---|---|---|---|---|-------|
| **R1749** | 1,145 | | | | | | | **1,145** |
| **R1774** | 1,171 | | | | 2,729 | | | **3,900** |
| **R1780** | 1,166 | | | | 2,662 | | | **3,828** |
| **R1784** | 1,247 | 1,884 | 3,242 | 3,355 | 2,675 | 2,819 | 526 | **15,748** |
| **R1789** | 1,307 | | | | 2,867 | | | **4,174** |
| **R1796** | | | | | 2,864 | | | **2,864** |
| **R1802** | 1,309 | | | | 2,184 | | | **3,493** |
| **R1806** | 1,333 | | | | 2,308 | | | **3,641** |
| **R1818** | 1,341 | 1,997 | 4,344 | 3,649 | 2,872 | 2,827 | 607 | **17,637** |
| **Total** | **10,019** | **3,881** | **7,586** | **7,004** | **21,161** | **5,646** | **1,133** | **56,430** |

**Table 3.33 Sources of rate book data**

**1749** WAC  Poor rate, St Anne King Square ward (1749), A/189; Poor rate, St Anne Leicester Fields ward (1749), A/190.

**1774** WAC Watch rate, St Anne King Square ward (1774), A/1526; Watch rate, St Anne Leicester Fields ward (1774), A/1527; Poor, highway and scavenger rate, St Margaret Grand ward (1774), E/471; Poor, highway and scavenger rate, St Margaret Absey ward (1774), E/472; Poor, highway and scavenger rate, St John (1774), E/473.

**1780** WAC Watch rate, St Anne King Square ward (1780), A/1549; Watch rate, St Anne Leicester Fields ward (1780), A/1550; Poor, highway and scavenger rate, St Margaret Grand ward (1780), E/492; Poor, highway and scavenger rate, St Margaret Absey ward (1780), E/493; Poor, highway and scavenger rate, St John (1780), E/494.

**1784** WAC Poor rate, St Anne King Square ward east (1784), A/326; Poor rate, St Anne King Square ward west (1784), A/327; Poor rate, St Anne Leicester Fields ward east (1784), A/328; Poor rate, St Anne Leicester Fields ward west (1784), A/329; Poor rate, St Clement (1784), B/203; Poor and highway rate, St George Conduit Street, Dover Street and Out wards (1784) C/361; Poor and highway rate, St George Grosvenor Street and Brook Street wards (1784), C/380; Poor, highway and scavenger rate, St Margaret Grand ward (1784), E/504; Poor, highway and scavenger rate, St Margaret Absey ward (1784), E505; Poor, highway and scavenger rate, St John (1784), E/506; Poor rate, St James (1784), D/105; Poor rate, St Martin (1784), F/584; Poor rate, St Mary (1784), G/190; Poor rate, St Paul (1784), H/112.

**1789** WAC Poor rate, St Anne King Square ward east (1789), A/394; Poor rate, St Anne King Square ward west (1789), A/395; Poor rate, St Anne Leicester Fields ward east (1789), A/396; Poor rate, St Anne Leicester Fields ward west (1789), A/397; Poor, highway and scavenger rate, St Margaret Grand ward (1789), E/527; Poor, highway and scavenger rate, St Margaret Absey ward (1789), E/328; Poor, highway and scavenger rate, St John (1789), E/329.

**1796** WAC Poor, highway and scavenger rate, St Margaret Grand ward (1796), E/548; Poor, highway and scavenger rate, St Margaret Absey ward (1796), E/549; Poor, highway and scavenger rate, St John (1796), E/550.

**1802** WAC Poor rate, St Anne Leicester Fields ward west (1802), A/522; Poor rate, St Anne King Square ward east (1802), A/523; Poor rate, St Anne King Square ward west (1802-3), A/525; Poor rate, St Anne Leicester Fields ward east (1802-3), A/526; Poor, highway and scavenger rate, St Margaret Grand ward (1802), E/566; Poor, highway and scavenger rate, St Margaret Absey ward (1802), E/567; Poor, highway and scavenger rate, St John (1802), E/568.

**1806** WAC Poor rate, St Anne King Square ward east (1804), A/550; Poor rate, St Anne King Square ward west (1804), A/551; Poor rate, St Anne Leicester Fields ward east (1804), A/552; Poor rate, St Anne Leicester Fields ward west (1804), A/553; Poor, highway and scavenger rate, St Margaret Grand ward (1806), E/578; Poor, highway and scavenger rate, St Margaret

Absey ward (1806), E/579; Poor, highway and scavenger rate, St John (1806), E/580.

**1818**  WAC Watch rate, St Anne King Square ward (1818), A/1696; Watch rate, St Anne Leicester Fields ward (1818), A/1697; Poor rate, St Clement (1818), B/241; Poor, watch and paving rate, St George Conduit Street ward (1819), C/420; Poor, watch and paving rate, St George Out ward (1819), C/469; Poor, watch and paving rate, St George Grosvenor Street ward (1819), C/519; Poor, watch and paving rate, St George Dover Street ward (1819), C/566; Poor, watch and paving rate, St George Brook Street ward (1819), C/614; Poor, watch and paving rate, St George Curzon Street ward (1819), C/636; Poor rate, St James (1819), D/139; Poor, highway and scavenger rate, St Margaret Grand ward (1819), E/623; Poor, highway and scavenger rate, St Margaret Absey ward (1819), E/624; Poor, highway and scavenger rate, St John (1819), E/625; Poor rate, St Martin (1819), F/652; Poor rate, St Mary (1819), G/304; Poor rate, St Paul (1818), H/168.

## 3.3 Occupational code book

The table **Dictionary** contains an example of every character string found in the *Occup* field in the poll books, together with the four-level occupational code assigned to it and described in greater detail in Chapter 4.5 below. These occupational character strings naturally contain all variant spellings (including typographical errors), and so considerably exceed the 1,612 distinct *Oclv4* codes assigned to them. Occupational coding was undertaken after data entry, thus retaining intact the occupational character string. It is thus possible for users of the Database to amend the coding as they see fit. Indeed, the creators of the Database stress that the occupational classification they offer here is descriptive rather than prescriptive. However, the occupational codes are also embedded in the Database rather than purely a look-up table as this increases the speed of implementation of database queries.

**Table 3.34 Standard format for Dictionary Table**

| Field Name | Description | Data Type | Field Length |
|---|---|---|---|
| **Occup** | Occupation string of voter as recorded in poll book | Character | 50 |
| **Oclv4** | Revised Booth/Armstrong classification of occupation of the voter as recorded in poll book | Character | 8 |
| **Oclv3** | Revised Booth/Armstrong classification of occupational trade cluster of the voter | Character | 7 |
| **Oclv2** | Revised Booth/Armstrong classification of occupational sub-sector of the voter | Character | 4 |
| **Oclv1** | Revised Booth/Armstrong classification of occupational sector of the voter | Character | 1 |

## 3.4 Soundex coding

The Westminster Historical Database is provided with a Soundex coding to facilitate record linkage. One example of every surname string in the Database was taken and placed in a new table **Sounds**, together with its appropriate Russell Soundex code. Just as there are more occupational character strings in the field *Occup* than there are occupational codes in the field *Oclv4*, so there are more surname character strings in the field *Surname* than there are corresponding Soundex codes in the field *Scode*. Like the occupational codes, the Soundex codes were added after data entry, and similarly are embedded in the Database. Thus the **Sounds** table represents a step in the creation of the Database in which Soundex codes were added to extant surname character strings.

**Table 3.35 Standard format for Sounds Table**

| Field Name | Description | Data Type | Field Length |
|---|---|---|---|
| **Surname** | Surname string as recorded in poll or rate book | Character | 25 |
| **Scode** | Russell Soundex code of surname string | Character | 5 |

*Notes*

[1]     We are grateful to Matthew Woollard of the University of Essex, who furnished us with Soundex codes from the Kleio program.

[2]     The procedure, similar to that described by I. Winchester, 'The linkage of historical records by man and computer: techniques and problems', *Journal of Interdisciplinary History* (1970), pp. 107-24, is described in M. Thaller, *Kleio, a database system*, Halbgraue Reihe zur Historischen Fachinformatik, B11 (St Katharinen, 1993), pp. 126-8. Alternative surname-treatment strategies include the Guth algorithm, described in G. Guth, 'Surname spellings and computerized record linkage', *Historical Methods*, 10 (1976), pp. 10-19; and the NYSIIS code, described in J. Atack, F. Bateman and M.E. Gregson, '"Matchmaker, matchmaker, make me a match": a general personal computer-based matching program for historical research', *Historical Methods*, 25 (1992), pp. 63-4.

[3]     The anachronistic term 'by-election', first recorded in 1880, is used here to denote an election to fill a vacancy caused by death, appointment to office, resignation, expulsion, or succession or elevation to the peerage.

[4]     Historians have made much of the incidence of uncontested elections in the period, but might usefully distinguish between general elections and by-elections. Uncontested general elections were unusual in Westminster, with only three occurring between 1749 and 1820. By contrast, twelve of the fifteen by-elections in the period were uncontested. Westminster experienced frequent by-elections because it attracted as candidates the sort of men likely to be appointed to office (six instances) or called to the Upper House (four instances). Two of the contested by-elections were caused by appointment to office, whilst that of 1819 was precipitated by Romilly's suicide.

[5]     Representation of the People Act, 1969.

[6]     BL Twining papers, Add. MS 39,936, fo. 133.

[7]     The following sketch of the political history of Westminster owes much to the volumes of the *History of Parliament* (hereafter *Hist. Parl.*): R. Sedgwick (ed.), *The House of Commons, 1715-54* (2 vols, 1970); L.B. Namier and J. Brooke (eds), *The House of Commons, 1754-90* (3 vols, 1964); and R.G. Thorne (ed.), *The House of Commons, 1790-1820* (5 vols, 1986).

[8]     Granville Leveson Gower, Viscount Trentham (1721-1803).

[9] Sir George Vandeput, Bt (1723-1784). For the election of 1749, see N. Rogers, 'Aristocratic clientage, trade and independency: popular politics in pre-radical Westminster', *Past and Present*, 61 (1973), pp. 70-106, and idem, *Whigs and cities.*

[10] Hervey Redmond Morres, Viscount Mountmorres (c. 1743-1797). See I.R. Christie, 'The Wilkites and the general election of 1774', in idem, *Myth and reality in late eighteenth-century British politics* (1970), pp. 244-60.

[11] Charles Stanhope, Viscount Mahon (1753-97). He is noted in *Hist. Parl. 1754-90*, iii, p. 462 by virtue of his election for Chipping Wycombe in 1780.

[12] Hugh Percy, Lord Warkworth (1742-1817).

[13] Thomas Pelham Clinton, Lord Lincoln (1752-95).

[14] On the petitioning movement in general, see E.C. Black, *The Association: British extraparliamentary political organization, 1769-83* (Cambridge, Mass., 1963). The experience of the metropolitan movement in support of the American colonists is discussed in J. Sainsbury, *Disaffected patriots: London supporters of revolutionary America, 1769-82* (Gloucester, 1987). On the national movement see also I.R. Christie, *Wilkes, Wyvill and reform: the parliamentary reform movement in Britain, 1760-85* (1962).

[15] Hon. Charles James Fox (1749-1806). By far the most famous of Westminster's representatives, Fox has been the subject of many studies. Mitchell, *Charles James Fox* is a recent scholarly life.

[16] BL Minutes of the 'Westminster Committee of Association', 2 February 1780-11 July 1785, Add. MSS 38,593-5. It was to 'prepare the plan of an Association ... to support the laudable reform, and such other measures, as may conduce to restore the freedom of parliament'. It proposed electoral registration, voting by ballot, payment of MPs, and the abolition of their property qualification. Add. MS 38,593, fos. 43-4.

[17] Sir George Brydges Rodney (1719-92).

[18] J.E. Norton (ed.), *The letters of Edward Gibbon* (3 vols, 1956), ii, p. 251. Lord Lincoln was the name by which Thomas Pelham Clinton, candidate in 1774, was known in 1780. See G.E.C[okayne] (ed.), *The complete peerage* (13 vols, 1910-59), ix, pp. 533-4.

[19] J.R. Dinwiddy, 'Charles James Fox and the people', *History*, 55 (1970), p. 342. The politics of the period are examined in L.G. Mitchell, *Charles James Fox and the disintegration of the Whig party, 1782-94* (Oxford, 1971).

[20] Sir Cecil Wray, Bt (1734-1805).

21 Sir Samuel Hood, Bt, Lord Hood (1724-1816).

22 The Westminster election of 1784 was the most notorious of the period: noteworthy for the intensity of its campaigning; for its duration of forty days; for its polling of over 12,000 electors; and for the colourful canvassing of the Duchess of Devonshire. A full contemporary account containing much primary material is Anon., *History of the Westminster election, containing every material occurrence, from its commencement on 1 April, to the final close of the poll, on 17 May* (1784; 2nd edn, 1785).

23 A. Aspinall (ed.), *The later correspondence of George III* (5 vols, Cambridge, 1962-70), i, p. 52 cites estimates of the Treasury expenditure on Hood's campaign in 1784 as £20,000, which was paid off over many years. The scrutiny is dealt with in P. Kelly, 'Pitt *versus* Fox: the Westminster scrutiny, 1784-5', *Studies in Burke and his time*, 14 (1972-3), pp. 155-62.

24 Hon. John Townshend (1757-1833).

25 John Horne Tooke (1736-1812). He is noticed in *Hist. Parl. 1790-1820*, iv, pp. 235-7 by virtue of his election for Old Sarum in 1801.

26 Sir Alan Gardner, Bt, Lord Gardner (1742-1808).

27 *Hist. Parl. 1790-1820*, ii, p. 268. Graham told the electors that 'it would not disgrace you to send a man of business to parliament'. Anon., *The picture of parliament* (1802), p. 83. A member of the firm of Graham and Hindle, auctioneers, and of Wright and Graham, sheriff's brokers, John Graham corresponded with Sheridan (whom he may also have known professionally).

28 Richard Brinsley Butler Sheridan (1751-1816). See also Anon., *History of the Westminster and Middlesex elections, in the month of November, 1806* (1807).

29 Sir Samuel Hood (1762-1814).

30 James Paull (1770-1808). He is noticed in *Hist. Parl. 1790-1820*, iv, pp. 733-5 by virtue of his election for Newport, Isle of Wight, in 1805.

31 Sir Francis Burdett, Bt (1774-1844). See M.W. Patterson, *Sir Francis Burdett and his times, 1770-1844* (2 vols, 1931) and, more recently, J.R. Dinwiddy, 'Sir Francis Burdett and Burdettite radicalism', *History*, 65 (1980), pp. 17-31.

32 A brief guide to the Westminster elections of the early nineteenth century is J.M. Main, 'Radical Westminster, 1807-20', *Historical Studies* (Australia and New Zealand), 12 (1965-7). For the election of 1807 see Anon., *An exposition of the circumstances which gave rise to the election of Sir Francis Burdett, Bt, for the City of Westminster* (1807).

33    Thomas Cochrane, Lord Cochrane (1775-1860). See C. Lloyd, *Lord Cochrane, seaman, radical, liberator: a life of Thomas, Lord Cochrane, 10th Earl of Dundonald* (1947).

34    Henry Hunt (1773-1835). See J. Belchem, *'Orator' Hunt: Henry Hunt and English working-class radicalism* (Oxford, 1985).

35    Hon. Douglas James William Kinnaird (1788-1830). He is noticed in *Hist. Parl. 1790-1820*, iv, pp. 340-41 by virtue of his election for Bishop's Castle in 1819.

36    John Cartwright (1740-1824). His long career in radical politics is examined in J. Osborne, *John Cartwright* (Cambridge, 1972).

37    Sir Samuel Romilly (1757-1818). Modern biographies include P. Medd, *Romilly: a life of Sir Samuel Romilly, lawyer and reformer* (1968).

38    Sir Murray Maxwell (1775-1831).

39    John Cam Hobhouse (1786-1869). See R.E. Zegger, *John Cam Hobhouse: a political life, 1819-52* (Columbia, Mo., 1973).

40    Hon. George Lamb (1784-1834).

41    A contemporary though partisan account of the election of 1819 is Anon., *An authentic narrative of the events of the Westminster election* (1819). A more judicious appraisal is W. Thomas, 'Radical Westminster' in idem, *The philosophic radicals: nine studies in theory and practice, 1817-41* (Oxford, 1979), pp. 46-94.

42    Anon., *The poll book ... for the City and Liberty of Westminster*, (1818), frontispiece. This print by Cruickshank entitled 'Westminster election' is described in George, ix, p. 810. Another representation of the hustings, *A scene at the new theatre, Covent Garden* (George, no. 6,536) is reproduced on the front of this volume.

43    The *pro-forma* poll book, of about 40 pages, had 18 lines to a page, although the number of voters recorded in each book was less than the theoretical maximum of 720 a book because of bad votes, prefatory matter, and space left at the completion of a day's polling.

44    LMA WR/PP/1788/1-3, and LMA Westminster poll books (1819), WR/PP/1819/1-4.

45    WAC Westminster poll books (1796), E/3081A.

46    Guildhall MS poll book for Westminster, 1796. This volume, from the library of Sir Alan Gardner, suggests that party managers took a close interest in the voting of their opponents.

47    LMA WR/PP/1788/23.

48    Guildhall MS poll book for Westminster, 1784.

[49]     Anon., *Guide to British historical manuscripts in the Huntington Library* (San Marino, Ca., 1982), p. 307. We are grateful to Bill Speck for drawing our attention to this source.

[50]     The parish of St John was rated with the neighbouring St Margaret, and is treated here as a ward of the latter parish with which its inhabitants polled.

[51]     The total of 15,648 items in the rate book database for 1784 may be compared with the figures given in 1789. This showed a total of 16,394 inhabited houses, of which 1,845 were headed by women. PRO 30/8/237, fo. 784. Some of the discrepancy may be explained by the splitting of the rates on business partnerships to form two or more records; another source of discrepancy lies in the fact that, when the statuses of female householders had been deleted it was then impossible to determine that she was indeed a woman. Mary Smith in the rate book would be deleted as an identifiable woman, but Mrs Smith would remain in the database as 'Smith'. Finally, because some people were rated on more than one property, these figures overestimate the number of householders.

# 4

# Occupational Classification

The Westminster Historical Database contains extensive information on occupations. For the purposes of analysis, this information has been classified using a multi-level coding system which is new and represents substantial added value to the Database. Such an exercise in turn raises a number of problems, which form the subject-matter of this chapter. In sequence, the discussion here considers: the general problems inherent in the exercise of classification; the nature of social classification when applied to historical data; the economic classification of pre-industrial and industrial societies; adaptations to the commonly-used Booth/Armstrong classification; the occupational classification scheme that augments the Westminster Historical Database; and, lastly, a brief conclusion stipulating the essential requirements for systems of socio-economic classification in application to historical data.

## General problems of classification

Assessment of the meaning of occupations in past societies has always required much care; and any formal system of classification multiplies the difficulties.[1] Criticism is highly likely to follow, as the exercise is hazardous from the start. Economic and social labels are often fluid and mutable, not readily identified or standardised. Historians therefore have to trample over subtleties when they wish to establish social and economic classifications.

Yet such a procedure is unavoidable for many purposes. Historical individuals, viewed with a close focus are undoubtedly and irreducibly individual. They do not always fit neatly into 'sectors' of an economy or into clear-cut class groupings. It is possible therefore to make a principled objection to any form of social labelling on these grounds. In the early 1830s, the young Harriet Martineau and the venerable S.T. Coleridge had a dispute on pre-

cisely this point. He reproached her: 'You appear to consider that
society is an aggregate of individuals!'; to which she replied: 'I
certainly did'.[2] In fact, Coleridge was himself no exponent of class
war. Yet his own soaring transcendentalism was based upon an
awareness of the 'many sided fact of an organised human society'.
Moreover, even the combative Martineau found it difficult to sus-
tain a position of pure individualism. Thus, in her economic text-
books, she too described contemporary society in terms of the rival
interests of 'Capital' and 'Labour'.

No analysis can, in practice, avoid using at least some aggregative or generalising concepts. When writing about societies in the
mass, it is not possible to proceed by summing them up individual
by individual. That would take far too much time – even to describe a community of hundreds, let alone one of millions – and
anyway this would still evoke some sort of summary at the end.
Similarly, even when the analytical focus is restricted to a single
person, it is difficult to avoid some generalising statements about
the social milieu in which that individual operated.

Moreover, larger classifications have an analytical identity and
rationale of their own. These may be valid, despite individual
exceptions. They are generic or generalising concepts, not simply
the sum of many case histories. Indeed, it is not unknown for some
strong organising ideas to be simultaneously powerful in broad-
brush application but fuzzy at close quarters. For example, the
'distributive' sector of an economy may be rightly distinguished
from the 'manufacturing' sector for economic analysis, even if
numerous individuals actually worked in occupations that crossed
the sectoral boundary. Many small shopkeeper/craftsmen in history
have sold as well as made their wares. Among many examples, the
'hatter' is a famous case in point, since in normal English usage
that term might apply to either a maker or a vendor of headgear –
or, of course, to one who was both.[3] Yet the fact that individuals
freely and frequently transgressed these notional boundaries does
not in any way preclude analysis of the agricultural, commercial,
manufacturing and service sectors of an economy. Both the
plurality of individual experiences and the clarity of formal
modelling are justifiable perspectives. However, it does mean that
generalising concepts have to be chosen and used with care. That
has long been one message hammered home by historians. The past
should not be confined into analytical categories that are either too

rigid or simply anachronistic.

Wherever possible, concepts and classifications should be fitting and adapted to the societies which they purport to illuminate. Indeed, from time to time generalisations lose their universal resonance and are quietly dropped or sidelined from the litany. 'Capitalism' as a stage in history is currently falling into analytical limbo. Its dates and definitions no longer command universal agreement. Thus while 'capitalism' is still strongly invoked by some historians of early modern Europe, others writing on the same period ignore the concept totally: it has become an analytical option rather than an inescapable stage of history.[4] Thus universalising categories are not immune themselves to questioning, adaptation, and sometimes rejection. There is a constant interplay between the general and the specific. Historians must therefore pay attention not only to the problems within any system of classification but also to the nature of any organising schema that is proposed.

These points are vividly illustrated in the case of data about occupations in past societies. Often the historian has nothing more than a simple occupational designation, without further information about the sort of work that was actually carried out by the individual in question. It was not unknown for people to vary their self-description on different occasions and in different circumstances.[5] Moreover, many generalised terms were used that hide a multitude of diverse activities.

Especially among the very poor, an 'economy of makeshift' encouraged individuals to turn their hand to whatever passing economic opportunities were available. Women were particularly susceptible to living by such means.[6] Indeed, it is widely acknowledged by historians that large amounts of casual work by female and child labour often went unrecorded. This is a perennial problem in studying work in past societies. The same also applied to many forms of seasonal employment. Of course, these complexities were rarely explained when people were asked to give themselves a simple label. A 'labourer' or 'shopkeeper' might play many economic roles, including some illicit ones which were never officially acknowledged as *bona fide* occupations. Indeed, no burglars, no receivers of stolen goods, no pimps, no prostitutes, no confidence tricksters ever appear in official listings of economic activity.[7]

Historians therefore need to approach the classification of occupations in history with a double caution. If problems cannot be eliminated, then at least pitfalls can be avoided. Hence both the apparent simplicity of occupational labels and the apparent lucidity of aggregative systems need to be scrutinised with great care – and, if need be, rejected. While classification is necessary, it does not follow that all classification systems are equally valid. Indeed, the reverse is true. Since systems of taxonomy so crucially affect patterns of thought and analysis, it becomes all the more important to check that classifications are valid both conceptually and in application.

## 4.2 Social classification

There are additional and considerable difficulties when attempting to attribute social status to individuals in past societies on the basis of occupational data without any other supporting information. It is all too easy for the hard-pressed historian to project backwards (often unconsciously) his or her own modern assumptions about the ranking of any particular form of work. But that is far too subjective and may positively mislead.

To take one example from an otherwise excellent study of the eighteenth-century urban electorate, O'Gorman groups woolcombers with labourers, tavern waiters and hawkers (and miscellaneous others) in the lowly category of 'labourers'.[8] In fact, however, many woolcombers were very wealthy men. They could be 'big masters' who organised the wholesale putting out of wool – and even the ordinary combers were skilled men at the top of the hierarchy of handicraft labour in terms of earnings.[9] Another occupation that poses problems of classification is that of the nineteenth-century 'engineer'. He may have been a skilled manual worker, among the labour aristocracy, working perhaps on the railways. Yet the term was rapidly diversifying in its social range.[10] Thus by the early nineteenth century it also referred to the technical experts who designed and built major construction works. These men were entering the skilled professions with rapidly increasing prestige and incomes to match.[11]

As these examples indicate there are evident dangers in deducing social status from work designations. How were occupations in the past ranked by contemporaries? And how did such attitudes either persist or change? Indeed, historians cannot assume that the same occupational labels always meant the same thing at different points in time. A 'manufacturer' in the early nineteenth century might refer simultaneously to a factory operative and to the factory owner.[12] But, by the twentieth century, the term had experienced a marked upwards drift and was confined to the large-scale capitalist producer.

Broadly speaking, it may be noted that the more generalised the terminology, the more difficult the task of classification becomes. A 'weaver' might have been anyone from a large master weaver, employing large numbers, to the poorest journeyman, eking out a living by working for others. The same applied to the 'shoemaker' and to any number of manufacturers, where no separate designations existed to differentiate between masters and men. Of course, some occupational labels were less problematic than others. A 'banker', for example, usually referred to someone from a fairly homogeneous group of relatively high status individuals. Conversely, a 'labourer' was generally found towards the lower reaches – though not necessarily at the very foot – of the social ladder. An exercise to investigate the taxable status of the Westminster electorate has confirmed that assumption.[13] Three quarters of those voters described as 'labourers' in 1818, who were linked successfully with individuals in the rate books,[14] were found to fall into the lowest quintile of rate assessments. The quarter who appeared somewhat more affluent were in the minority.

Things were not so clear, however, for the many occupations between these polarities. The same micro-study of the Westminster electorate in the later eighteenth century shows that a number of occupations were spread between the rateable bands. Builders and tailors, for example, were distributed fairly uniformly across the scale of assessments. They were not predominantly rich, middling or poor; but diffused across the spectrum. Hence, while some social groups appeared relatively homogeneous in rate-paying terms (bricklayers, carpenters, labourers), others were not at all (builders, tailors).

Of course, rateable assessments may constitute a fair guide to the value of housing but they offer only a crude proxy for wealth. Nor do capital assets alone (assuming that information is available) constitute the final arbiter of social position. The source of income as well as its quantity has a crucial bearing upon public esteem.

Moreover, it is difficult to discover the full details of individual wealth in history, especially as allowances also have to be made for the normal fluctuations in affluence during the life-cycle. One possible compromise might be to weight occupations to indicate mean wealth per occupation. Yet such supporting information is extremely difficult to find. Mean values might also simultaneously. conceal a wide variation in incomes or wealth-holdings.[15]

The implication is that simple occupational labels are often too opaque to function as adequate indicators of social status on their own, without additional information or corroboration from some other independent source. Directories, tax records, and other local sources may offer additional documentation. But the creation of plural indicators of social status is far from an easy matter. Multivariate analysis will thus undoubtedly make more work for historians. It will also serve to make social classification less problematic and it can introduce a more dynamic element into the analysis. However, it will not resolve all the difficulties. Certainly, the modern trend in historical research has quite rightly thrown doubt on all simple 'clumpings' of data into static categories, whether of 'class', 'status', 'neighbourhood' or 'community'.[16] It follows that rigid classifications will always be open to criticism.

A further complexity is that far more information tends to survive about male than female occupations. As a result, it is often simplistically assumed that women have the same social status as their spouses, thereby making it impossible to study (for example) inter-class marriage patterns. Indeed, this difficulty illustrates a central concern when devising social indices. It is crucial to ensure that the criteria for classification do not build the answers into the definitions. One example of this classic problem is to be found in S.A. Royle's pioneering study of mid-nineteenth-century social structure in three Leicestershire small towns (Coalville, Hinckley and Melton Mowbray).[17] He devised his own five-part social classification, in which the upper and middle classes were represented by groups I-III, the skilled working class became class IV and the unskilled class V. Households were then allocated into these categories using a variety of criteria. One of these was the employment of servants, which was deemed a characteristic of upper- and middle-class society (classes I-III). The results were conclusive. Absolutely none of the working class (IV or V) employed domestic servants. Yet it was not necessary to survey hun-

dreds of households to discover that, since – rightly or wrongly –
the conclusion was built into the classification.

York society in 1851 provides a dramatic contrast with that
result. There Armstrong's five-fold classification, based solely upon
occupational criteria, found servant-keeping households stretched
well beyond the upper and middle classes (I-II) into the lower
social classes III-IV, albeit with a preponderance of such households among classes I-II.[18] But again that may suggest that there
are implausibilities in this system of classification too. It means that
social classes are not simply 'out there' waiting to be discovered.
The historian's decisions about classification will crucially affect the
outcome.

Additional problems are posed by the difficulty of identifying the
number of significant classes or social groupings into which the
data are to be organised. The more sub-divisions that are selected,
the greater the uncertainties when allocating occupations and the
greater the potential for error. Conversely, the simpler the model,
the greater the likelihood of blurring genuine social distinctions and
of producing unhelpful or even meaningless results. A two-fold
division of society into 'great' and 'small' or 'rich' and 'poor'
would ease classification in one sense, since the range of options
are dramatically narrowed. On the other hand, a binary typology
creates fresh difficulties in allocating 'middling' occupations and
results in the continuing analytical invisibility of a social group
whose importance has often been quite unjustly overlooked.[19]

If, however, a plurality of classes or social groupings is required,
what should their number be? Did the significant social divisions
remain constant over time? Have they become more or less complex as societies have gradually become commercialised and indus-
trialised? In modern Britain, there has been no consensus. Three,
sometimes four, or five classes have all been proposed by different
experts,[20] whilst in 1814, for example, the knowledgeable social
commentator Patrick Colquhoun analysed seven.[21] Some modern
historians argue against any at all.[22] The conspicuous lack of
agreement about something as basic as the number of significant
social groupings indicates the intense subjectivity of the whole
question.

Five classes are often adopted by modern sociologists and
economists. Sometimes these are simply dubbed as numbers I-V.
Yet, increasingly, to avoid giving offence by reference to an overt

'top' and 'bottom' of the social ladder, they are known more chastely as social classes A-E. Sub-groups can then be added, so that, for example, C1 represents the skilled manual workers. In origin, the schema was suggested by the Registrar General for analysing British census results in 1911; and it has been subsequently refined from census to census, by moving different occupations up and down the scale while retaining the basic five-fold framework.[23] It was constructed as the outcome of prolonged arguments about the relationship between class and occupational morbidity.[24] The result then became enshrined, as Armstrong remarks in an aside, as 'the Whitehall civil servants' view of the social hierarchy'.[25]

Within this system, the classification attempted to allow for complexity at the margins. Hence the five grades consisted of three known social polarities and two 'intermediate' groupings between them, as follows:

**Table 4.1 The 1911 five-fold social classification**

| Class I | Upper and middle class |
| --- | --- |
| Class II | Intermediate between I and III (occupations like shopkeepers) |
| Class III | Skilled working class |
| Class IV | Intermediate between III and V (eg partially skilled occupations) |
| Class V | Unskilled working class |

Applying this to historical occupations, however, has multiplied the problems already inherent in any system of classification. The major difficulty is that it tends to produce a 'swollen' class III. Many industrial occupations have titles that imply some manufacturing expertise. Only relatively few indicated their status at work, especially if it was lowly. Thus Armstrong's study of York in 1851 found that as many as 49 per cent of all household heads fell into the category of skilled working class. Not surprisingly, critics have complained that this group is 'too large, unwieldy and undifferentiated'. Armstrong's answer to this criticism is to suggest that the skilled workforce could be sub-divided for analysis into different occupational sub-sections.[26] Meanwhile, other historians, using alternative occupational rankings, have managed to reduce the size of class III and to increase class II instead.[27] But here the possibilities of massaging the data to produce a pre-required outcome become ever more apparent.

Two famous 'boundary' designations highlight the problems of classifying individuals as members of the middle class. On the lower margins between respectability and the working class came the 'artisan'. In the nineteenth century, this term was quite widely used but rarely defined.[28] Was the 'artisan' an independent small master craftsman, just scraping into the ranks of the respectable middling sort? Or was he a skilled journeyman – working for others to earn his bread? Both usages can be found, with the latter tending to predominate as the term gradually moved 'down' the social scale. But at any given time, there are problems in classifying an artisan unless more is known about his way of life.

Just as puzzling, at the other end of the scale, was the social designation of the 'gentleman'.[29] This of course was not an occupational label. Rather, it was often given in lieu of that. But what did it mean? From the start, it was not applied exclusively to landowners. Usage was eclectic and inventive. In Westminster in 1749 one self-styled gentleman was described as being 'miserable poor, almost naked', while another was said to keep a bawdy house.[30] Status also varied with age and life cycle. In 1784 one Samuel Collins of Westminster described himself as a rubbish carter; in 1788 and 1796 he was a scavenger; and in 1802 (assuming that he was indeed the same person) he had become a gentleman, at least to his own satisfaction.[31]

Less problematically, by the eighteenth century, plenty of respectable urban professional and mercantile men called themselves gentlemen – and were so called by others – perfectly legitimately and without contention. How then should they be categorised? They were staples of urban society. Yet not all were simply 'middling'. Some were great urban plutocrats. How then was the floating concept of the gentleman to be classified? Certainly, not simply as a landowner. Nor simply as a member of the urban elite. He might be urban or rural, grandee or middling. Each case needs careful scrutiny on its own merits.

Difficulties can be sidestepped if the upper and middle classes are grouped together (as in Table 4.1 above). But this may be far too reductionist for most analytical purposes. For some purposes it is important to be able to distinguish between the nuances of life at the top and in the middle. But that can only be done with good, detailed evidence. Indeed, it is fraught with problems to analyse the

'rise of the middle class' on the strength of occupational data
alone, not least in England because of the amorphous role of the
'gentleman'.[32]

Generalised designations should thus be deployed to provide
social classifications with great caution and only if absolutely required. On their own, they are often imprecise indicators of class or
ranking, especially for the many in the 'middling' strata. The no-
bleman and the beggar may be relatively easy to distinguish, but in
a non-caste society the swathes of population between them were
generally not clearly differentiated by label. Multiple indices of
social position should be deployed wherever feasible, and as systematically as possible, to supplement occupational listings. As
demonstrated above, for example, information about rateable or
taxable status can sometimes be used to throw light upon individual
status.

Modern communities can furthermore provide additional data
relating to the subjective ranking of any given occupation. Public
attitudes can be canvassed to construct indices of commonly accepted social prestige. Yet, even here, great care is required. Status
designations and assumptions are mutable. Occupational rankings
may quickly become out of date, leaving historians with ossified
systems.[33] Hence it is important that connotations of social
'prestige' also be subject to reclassification as required.

Clearly, then, it is essential, as a matter of good practice, that all
the assumptions underlying any system that groups occupations
into a ranked hierarchy should be made apparent at all times – and
that is especially crucial when the social classification has been
based upon pure occupational designations without any supporting
information to uphold an attributed ranking.[34] As a result, most
modern assessments try to retain as much internal flexibility as
possible, a process that is aided by the flexibility of modern computer coding systems.

Alternatively, too, these problems can be taken as historical
evidence in their own right. Thus it can be argued instead that the
breadth of many occupational designations tended in itself to blur
rigid boundaries of class identification. Thus a generalised and
indeed accurate belief that there was a social hierarchy could be
held in tandem with a horizontal occupational identification, cutting
across vertical rankings. Such pluralism is certainly upheld by the
fact that, in most non-caste societies, people outside the nobility

were not publicly ranked in terms of status.

Ultimately, of course, historians cannot and should not avoid social generalisations. But they need to be aware of the overlapping meanings behind apparently innocent aggregates. When collective generalisations are deployed, they should always be defined clearly. And when the argument becomes specific and turns upon precise percentages, historians should especially realise that elaborate systems of social classification based upon occupations alone are more than usually fallible.

## 4.3 Economic classification

Classification for economic analysis is slightly less contentious but still poses a large number of problems. Occupational titles were, after all, indicators of an individual's legitimate role in the workplace. The terminology was sometimes generalised and inexact but it had a meaning for contemporaries. It is, however, the classification and interpretation of such data that creates difficulties, and the problems are compounded when attempts are made at systematic international comparisons.[35]

Of course, the historian is here studying information as it was recorded on the public record. There is no way of guaranteeing that individuals were currently active in the occupation by which they were known. People may have been out of work or engaged in some other form of labour or erroneously reported. Indeed, as noted above, it was not unknown for the same individual to be described in different ways in different circumstances and different sets of records. Such flexibility of nomenclature was perfectly legitimate.

Furthermore, it was not unknown to carry out a secondary occupation alongside that declared. A weaver might also keep an alehouse; a nailer work on his small farm; and so forth. And entrepreneurs often invested simultaneously in trade, industry, land and transport. As R.J. Morris points out, 'this was a wise way of spreading risk in a very insecure economy'.[36] Multiple occupations should always be recorded when they are known. After all, the range and number of such conjunctions is interesting information in itself. However, these parallel activities can only be traced when they leave a historical record, which they rarely do.

Hence the historian is well advised to check the source of any occupational label and to remain alert to the possibility of additions and alternatives. In particular, it is important to establish whether a given designation was provided by the individual in question or attributed by another; and, in the latter case, with what likelihood of accuracy.[37] But error and confusion can never be eliminated completely. Ultimately, the historian has to accept occupational descriptions for what they were: as plausible and public indicators of an individual's primary declarable relationship to the world of work (and sometimes of status) on one given occasion, rather than as absolutely perfect and permanent reflections of the wider economy to which they referred. It is not ideal. But historians habitually work with data as they are rather than as they might be.

Aggregative analysis also involves other assumptions. In practice, it is impossible to know if a 'hatter' in Norwich did the same work as a 'hatter' in Shrewsbury. But the spread of a common vocabulary and the gradual disappearance of separate dialect terms at least implies that there was some recognisable common ground.[38] And that process of national standardisation was greatly accelerated from 1841 onwards, when the national census began collecting and summarising information about occupations. Many thousands of local terms were rapidly subsumed into standard categories. Indeed, after 1861 a regularly-updated dictionary of terminology was issued to the clerks in the census office, so that they could turn the multiplicity of titles into a systematic classification for general perusal.[39] Again, it implied that local and industrial variants were comprehensible within a national schema. Thus historians generally follow suit and assume a degree of compatibility in terminology between regions, except in the case of accepted variants – and also over time, again excepting those working names that are known to have significantly changed in meaning.

That said, occupational labels referred to known forms of economic activity, which can be analysed aggregatively. However, further problems arise in choosing an appropriate system of classification. Ideally, it would be helpful to look at the structure of employment by differentiating master from apprentice, mistress from maidservant, capitalist employer from waged employee. In a few fields, that can be done. Living-in servants were habitually identified within the domestic hierarchy by the nomenclature of their service occupations.

Outside the household, however, things were far from clear. As already noted, British occupational designations very rarely made any linguistic reference to status within work. When describing themselves in the nineteenth-century census returns, for example, people generally avoided reference to terms such as 'journeymen', 'hands' or 'employees'.[40] And that tradition had a long history. European occupational terminology generally pointed to the general field of work rather than the employment status of the worker within that. Only from the mid-twentieth century onwards did the British census attempt to record systematically both personal occupation and industrial role.[41] Economic hierarchy thus cannot be inferred from unvarnished occupational labels, except in certain specified environments such as the servant-employing household and even that depends upon the workforce being reported in full and rich detail rather than simply as 'servants'.

More promising, however, are the possibilities of analysing occupations within the relevant sectors of the economy. The nature of work is more readily identified than the problematics of status at work and ranking within the wider society. Even here, however, things still remain far from simple. What sectoral groupings are to be used? And can or should the same aggregations be used over long periods of time? If the groupings do remain constant, then longitudinal comparisons are facilitated. On the other hand, that technique may easily obscure significant shifts in economic organisation over time. As a result of that perception, the search for a universal coding of occupations has generally been abandoned by economic historians.[42] However, within a given timespan and economic typology, there is a case for some degree of systematisation to facilitate comparison.

Ideal in many ways would be a simple but clear taxonomy that allocated the workforce respectively into the primary (agricultural), secondary (manufacturing) and tertiary (commercial and service) sectors of the economy. Some now add a 'quaternary' division to encompass those employed in governmental and administrative occupations. These groupings certainly make conceptual sense. And as such they provide a valid tool for macro-economic analysis, as it is well established that developing economies tend to shift their workforce from the primary into the secondary and tertiary sectors.

Practically, however, it is virtually impossible to allocate all historic occupations with confidence into these distinctive sectors, especially in the case of pre-modern economies which did not have a high degree of job specialisation. Individual workers often straddled the boundaries. They were not, after all, required to allocate themselves into one specific sector. Thus before the advent of modern networks of mass storage and distribution, local farmers often took their produce to market for sale directly to consumers. That meant that the boundaries between the agricultural and commercial sectors were not rigid.

More crucially still, for long periods of history manufacturing and retailing occupations were not mutually exclusive. This was an important qualification, since large numbers within the workforce found themselves straddling this boundary. It meant that the distinction between the secondary and tertiary sectors, while clear-cut analytically, was not at all obvious in the case of individual workers. As already noted, a 'hatter' might be either a maker or vendor of headgear or, very possibly, both. The same applied to many other small manufacturers, before the advent of modern mass production.[43] In other words, there was no authority that insisted that 'makers' should do nothing but 'make'. They often retailed goods of their own manufacture – with perfect economic rationality and social acceptability.

It is difficult therefore for the historian to avoid an element of arbitrary judgement. Any system of occupational classification that attempts to provide broad sectoral groupings faces these problems, especially on the boundary between secondary and tertiary economic activities. If everyone who is termed a 'maker' is placed into secondary production, that understates the extent of retailing. If conversely everyone who might possibly be a retailer or trader is grouped automatically into the tertiary sector, then manufacturing production can be reduced dramatically since many 'makers' might also have been vendors.

Too stark a rubric, one way or the other, can in effect skew the results to fit into a predetermined conclusion. The best the historian can do is to 'play fair' with the data, and then to recall that, in all but the most modern and specialised economies, the 'manufacturing' sector always included some 'tertiary' activities and *vice versa*. In other words, all classifications have fuzzy edges. As a result, these most global of aggregations do not always provide the most helpful focus for economic analysis.

Some systems therefore avoid the broadest sectoral groupings entirely. Instead, they focus upon linked groups of occupation that are aggregated by type of product or service rather than by macro-economic function. These systems are often applied to medieval and early modern data, when the division between manufacturing and tertiary employment was unclear. Examples of 'product' groupings that are often invoked are: 'food and drink', 'minerals', 'construction', 'clothing'. The latter is sometimes indicated as 'clothing and textiles' or sometimes with 'textiles' separately in areas with substantial woollen industries and hence a large specialist weaving workforce. Similarly, examples of 'service' groupings are: 'professions', 'services' (often domestic), 'finance' and sometimes 'merchants'. But again there is no standard format here and no universal agreement of where individual occupations are allocated.

Problems arise especially when status and economic categories are mixed together. It is possible to preselect within an urban population a 'middle' class (usually the gentlemen plus the professions) while the rest are put into a hierarchy of trades. But that is highly misleading. Some at least of the dealers and manufacturers (for example, eminent grocers or master weavers) might well have been members of the urban elite. Under such a system, however, they remain humbly grouped into 'trades'. And the size and composition of the elite is misleadingly indicated. It remains unwise therefore to try to make one classification serve simultaneously as an indicator of social status and of economic role.

Contrasting examples from two studies published in the 1980s highlight the problems both of classification and of comparability (Table 4.2).[44] Both groupings have problems, although they were constructed to deal with rather different sets of data. The classification in column A is rather thin on categories. Transport and the professions, for example, are lost from view. Furthermore, it is not clear where a 'merchant' would be grouped. And the large-scale production of textiles has disappeared since it is subsumed into the same category as dressmakers and milliners (that is also a problem in Column B). Moreover, the economic role of the gentlemen is far from clear. In practice they could also have been farmers or professional men as well as landowners living off their rentals. (But presumably the classification lacked additional information to 'decode' this opaque status label).

**Table 4.2 Examples of classification schemes**

GALENSON                                ELLIS

| Column A | Column B |
| --- | --- |
| **Mixed status/product** | **Mixed sector/product** |
| Gentlemen | |
| Farmers | Agriculture |
| Food and drink | Food and drink |
| Metal and construction | Minerals, construction |
| Textiles and clothing | Textiles and clothing, Animal and vegetable products _Split_ |
| Services | Services, Professions, Commerce and transport |
| Labourers _Split_ | Miscellaneous [includes gentlemen, labourers, and beggars] |
| Not stated | Not known |

The classification scheme in column B is much more carefully differentiated, although it too does not distinguish large-scale textile production from the making and retailing of clothing. It also has some curious features of its own. The grouping of 'commerce' with 'transport' seems odd. The category of 'animal and vegetable products' seems very odd – since many of its entrants could equally well be grouped under 'food and drink' or under 'textiles and clothing'. And, above all, the 'miscellaneous' category of 'gentlemen, labourers and beggars' seems to defy any known social or economic rationale.

Neither column A nor column B of Table 4.2, it may be noted, intends to differentiate strictly between the secondary and tertiary sectors of the economy. They are concerned instead to highlight the relevant occupational clusters within their own data. This they do, although not in a manner that makes comparison between the two studies very easy. Given these pitfalls, therefore, historians should always clarify their criteria for classification. Key decisions should not be left for readers to take on trust. In addition, computerised coding systems should always retain the ability to return to the original occupational designation. Any classification can then be amended swiftly and simply, if need arises, without causing major intellectual or practical upheavals. Commonly used groupings are listed below in Table 4.3, but there are many variants in use.[45]

**Table 4.3 Common classificatory groups for early modern occupations**

Leisured (landowners)
Professions
Food and Drink/Victualling
Household Goods
Distributive Trades
Clothing
Textiles
Leather
Building and Furnishings (furnishings sometimes with clothing)
Transport
Agriculture/Rural
Labourers

In particular, having reviewed all this diversity, it follows that historians should be wary of inventing their own systems *de novo*, especially without a background in socio-economic history and an appreciation of the nuances of occupational nomenclature. There is too great a risk of projecting modern assumptions backwards into history, as well as further multiplying the current variety of non-comparable systems. Instead, there are various semi-standard classifications for specific periods of history which can generally be used or adapted. As stated earlier, however, it is neither desirable nor possible to confine all classifications into one standard format that its true for all countries, all climes and all eras. The past and present diversity of practice seems certain to ensure that pluralism will continue.[46]

## 4.4 Adapting the Booth/Armstrong classification

Nineteenth-century occupational titles are commonly classified using the system known by the names of Booth and Armstrong. These were the pioneers who respectively compiled and adapted this tabulation. Booth himself drew it from the Registrar General's classification in the mid-nineteenth century.[47] It is neither perfect nor foolproof. Nor is it universally applicable. It must be stressed therefore that the comments that follow emphatically do not constitute an appeal for the global adoption of Booth/Armstrong. The discussion in this section seeks simply to highlight the relative strengths and weaknesses of the classification system; and to propose two critical restructurings to the Booth/Armstrong schema.

Booth/Armstrong is primarily an industrial classification that sub-divides occupations by type of product or service. Its focus is upon the nature of work. It does not, however, attempt to indicate a social or workplace hierarchy, since unvarnished occupational titles do not provide sufficient data for that (as demonstrated above). Thus it highlights fields of economic activity rather than status or workplace organisation within that. Nine major fields of employment are designated, each being divided into component activities – totalling 79 sub-fields. (There is no limit to the additional number of sub-fields that can be generated within this system). On the strength of that, Armstrong's updating of Booth proposed a twofold coding for each occupation. One indicator listed the major field and the second the sub-field. Furthermore, modern computer coding now allows a much more flexible approach than that envisaged by Armstrong in 1972. It is now generally accepted that a third notation or coding is added to the string. That indicates the original occupational title, as originally specified in the source.[48] New forms of work, that were not encountered by either Booth or Armstrong, can similarly be coded and allocated to a field and sub-field within the system.

Such a threefold arrangement allows for analysis at all three different levels of specification.[49] Crucially, too, it follows 'best practice' by permitting individual occupations to be readily reallocated into a different field or sub-field, within this overall schema, if so required. Flexibility is thus ensured. Indeed, there is nothing to prevent the reallocation of an entire sub-field, again should the need arise. Reconfiguration is always possible. Before itemising the strengths and weaknesses of this system, it is helpful to view a condensed tabulation of its major fields and sub-fields, as they range across the spectrum of types of production, distribution and services (see Table 4.4).

Despite its apparent faults, this classification has a certain logic. It is focused centrally upon economic categories and it aggregates the data into different levels of specialisation. Indeed, a strong feature of the classification is that it takes into account simultaneously the type of product, the raw materials used (if applicable) and the economic sector involved. It therefore incorporates the notion of sub-specialisms within broader categories.

On the strength of that, general assessments can thence be made of the nature, range and quantity of separate occupations; of the type, range and number of identifiable sub-fields; and of the balance between the major sectors. For example, it does allow the historian to analyse the relative importance of involvement in 'manufacturing' and 'dealing', so that it incorporates at least in principle some distinction between production and distribution. Another merit, though not unique to Booth/Armstrong, is the flexibility of the system. A wide range of post-1700 occupations can be accommodated within its maw. New fields and sub-fields can be created, if required. And new occupations, in the sense of those that had not been encountered by Booth or Armstrong, can readily be added.

Various difficulties, however, still remain. One is a very practical as well as theoretical problem. As general fields, the two sectors of 'manufacturing' and 'dealing' attract a large number of entries. Yet it remains problematic in a number of cases to classify occupations into one of those categories or the other. This happens because production and retailing were not necessarily differentiated (as already noted above). Where should, for example, a 'baker' be classified? Before the advent of modern mass production, he or she might well have worked both as a 'maker' and a 'dealer'. And the same problem recurs in the case of numerous other occupations, notably in the case of the manufacture and vending of food, drink, and small household items, such as clothing.

**Table 4.4 Major occupational groupings in Booth/Armstrong classification**

| Code | Major Field | Subgroups |
|------|-------------|-----------|
| **AG** | Agriculture/Fishing | Farming/land service |
| | | Fishing |
| **MI** | Mining | Mining |
| | | Quarrying |
| | | Brickmaking |
| **BU** | Building | Management |
| | | Operative |
| | | Road-making |

| Code | Major Field | Subgroups |
|------|-------------|-----------|
| **MF** | Manufacturing | Machinery/tool-making |
| | | Shipbuilding |
| | | Minerals (various) |
| | | Furniture/wood products |
| | | Paper |
| | | Woollens |
| | | Cottons and silk |
| | | Lace |
| | | Dress and related |
| | | Food/drink preparation |
| | | Watch/clocks |
| | | Numerous others |
| **TR** | Transport | Warehouse and docks |
| | | Ocean/inland navigation |
| | | Railways |
| | | Roads |
| **DE** | Dealing | Raw materials |
| | | Clothing materials/dress |
| | | Food/tobacco/drink |
| | | Household utensils |
| | | Furniture |
| | | General dealers |
| | | Others |
| **IS** | Industrial service | Banking/insurance |
| | | Labour (general) |
| **PP** | Public serv-ice/Professional | Central and local administration |
| | | Army/Navy |
| | | Prison service |
| | | Law |
| | | Medicine |
| | | Arts (various) |
| | | Education |
| | | Churches |
| **DS** | Domestic service | Indoor service |
| | | Outdoor service |
| | | Other services, eg. Hairdressing |

Arbitrary decisions are thus unavoidable in a certain number of cases. At least, however, they should be made consistently. In the case of the Booth/Armstrong classification, all occupations specifically named as 'makers' (such as boot- and shoe-makers) are classified as manufacturing. That gives the system overall a slight bias towards production, while at the same time it does attend closely to occupational nomenclature. Thus, for example, a 'hat-maker' and a 'hat-cutter' are taken to be manufacturers, while the famous 'hatter' is classified as a dealer. And so on. The 'baker' is assumed to be named as a contraction of 'bread-maker' and is thus a manufacturer, while the proprietor of a 'pastry-cake-shop' is a dealer.

Imperfect as all these compromises must be, they provide a basis for consistent classification. And it must always be remembered that each sectoral total of 'manufacturing' and 'dealing' indicates its minimum core rather than its total extent. Individuals did not fit neatly into analytical categories. Hence some dealing was always carried out by manufacturers and *vice versa*.

Similar difficulties can be found on the boundaries between other classifications. General 'warehousing' according to Booth/Armstrong is classified into the sector concerned with 'transport'. However, in a number of cases, the occupational title appears to indicate wholesale dealing rather than simply storage. That is made specific when the nature of the product is indicated. Hence all warehousing occupations that designated the commodity in question, such as 'tobacco- and snuff-warehouse' or 'china warehouse', were classified as 'dealing'. In practice, there may have been some overlap between those who sold goods and those who arranged for their transportation. Making decisions on the margins between classifications, however, remains unavoidable at the level of sectoral analysis (although the original occupations can be analysed on their own without worrying about these problems). Overall, the Booth/Armstrong system provides a wide-ranging conspectus of any given economy. Aggregative constructs such as agriculture, mining, building, manufacturing, transport, dealing, public service/professional, and domestic/personal service work well enough. For example, Armstrong provides two urban cases studies. He surveys occupations in Bath and Sheffield in 1861; and their overall classification not only look plausible but provide a number of leads for further analysis.[50]

Unfortunately, however, the ninth category proposed by Booth/

Armstrong proves pretty much of a hybrid. It is named as 'industrial service' and includes not only bankers, financiers and brokers but also general labourers and porters. This hybrid grouping does not have much real economic coherence. It sunders 'brokers' from 'merchants' brokers' who are classified as dealers. And it groups labourers with bankers, while 'brickmakers' labourers' appear separately within building. However, the field is generally retained for comparability, even while it cannot be said to constitute a very homogeneous grouping within the general classification.

Added to all these problems, occupational listings often included a number of status designations and honorific titles. These were used perfectly legitimately by individuals who identified themselves not by field of employment but by social ranking. A common example is the English 'gentleman'. In practice, as noted above, that title might cover a multitude of sins and virtues. It was both adopted by individuals and attributed by others – not always to the same effect. How should the gentleman and his lady be accommodated into the Booth/Armstrong classification? If he or she listed an occupation as well as an honorary title, then at least part of the problem was resolved, since the occupation would be given an appropriate classification.[51]

What should be the fate, however, of those individuals who cited nothing more than a status designation? There was no official place for that within the nine-fold groupings. On the other hand, the people with status designations were often sufficiently numerous that their role needed acknowledgement. Furthermore, it is not a good principle of research to discard potentially valuable historical information. The solution adopted for the Westminster Historical Database[52] has been to incorporate an additional economic, not social field. The titled population are listed as 'Rentiers' under the headcode RE. Again, this is not a perfect solution, since there is no guarantee that all 'gentlemen' were property-owners. It does, however, encourage a separate assessment of the economic role of the titled population, who otherwise would be left unclassified or merely grouped into 'miscellaneous'. Interestingly, moreover, this amendment reverts to a category of classification (as 'property-owning/independent') that was originally used by Booth but subsequently suppressed by Armstrong.[53] Revised in that way, the Booth/Armstrong classification then becomes ten-fold (plus a spare category for terminology that is too cryptic or obscure for classification):

**Table 4.5 Revised Booth/Armstrong classification**

| Code | Major Field |
| --- | --- |
| AG | Agriculture/Fishing |
| MI | Mining |
| BU | Building |
| MF | Manufacturing |
| TR | Transport |
| DE | Dealing |
| PP | Public service/Professional |
| IS | Industrial service |
| DS | Domestic service |
| RE | Rentiers |
| XX | Unidentified or Missing data |

RE — Rentiers — *GENTLEMAN STATUS DESIGNATION BASICALLY.*

## 4.5 Occupational classification in the Westminster Historical Database

A total of 1,612 distinct occupations were recorded in the poll books between 1749 and 1820.[54] This included slight differences of occupational description (oyster seller/oysterman), but excluded variant spellings (plaisterer/plasterer) and common contractions (attorney/attorney at law). However the distribution of voters within occupations was highly uneven: thousands of voters described themselves as gentlemen, tailors, carpenters, shoemakers and victuallers. But, whilst they are striking testimony to the scope for specialisation in the metropolitan economy, there was only one recorded dog doctor, only one bug destroyer, only one horse milliner, only one mousetrap maker, only one tomb shower, and only one water closet maker.[55] Westminster contained many artisans, craftsmen and shopkeepers, together with many gentry and professional men. The farmers were virtually absent by 1749, whilst the mineral extractive industries were represented by a solitary brick maker, who was re-classified among the Builders.

**Table 4.6 Breakdown of occupational classification in the Westminster Historical Database**

| Level 1 | Level 2 | Level 3 | Level 4 |
|---|---|---|---|
| Agriculture/Fishing | 3 | 10 | 15 |
| Building | 3 | 19 | 56 |
| Manufacturing | 31 | 154 | 672 |
| Transport | 4 | 12 | 44 |
| Dealing | 13 | 120 | 444 |
| Industrial service | 2 | 9 | 27 |
| Public service/Professional | 13 | 62 | 271 |
| Domestic service | 3 | 11 | 56 |
| Rentiers | 5 | 5 | 25 |
| Unallocatable | 1 | 1 | 1 |
| **Total** | **79** | **404** | **1,612** |

The economic sector with the greatest number of distinct trades was that of the Manufacturers, with 672, followed by the Dealers with 444 different callings, and the Professional men, with 271 different professional titles. Those giving status designations take the classification 'RE', representing a class of Rentiers. The classification of occupations, outlined below in Tables 4.6, 4.7 and 4.8 shows how the taxonomy operated hierarchically to subsume different categories. There are many ways of classifying occupations, and the taxonomy shown here is descriptive rather than prescriptive. It is based upon the amended Booth/Armstrong classification, as explained above. The category of 'Mining', which was not found in Westminster, was dropped. And throughout, an additional level of classification has been added to allow related trades to be grouped together: thus cordwainers and shoemakers share a common Level 3 classification. The fourfold classification thus follows Booth/Armstrong at Level 1, representing the sector of the economy, and at Level 2, representing the sub-sector. But to these are added Level 3, representing the grouped trades or occupations, and Level 4, representing the occupation as given in the poll book.

Occupational classifications must be mutually exclusive and exhaustive. Each occupation must be given a code, none may have more than one code, and no distinct occupations may share a common code. But the classification of occupations is far from straightforward. Booth proposed an occupational classification of 'those who produce raw material in various ways, and those who prepare it for use; those who distribute what is produced, and finally those who in other ways serve the community'.

**Table 4.7 Outline occupational classification in the Westminster Historical Database**

| Sector | Sub-sector | Description | Distinct occupations |
|--------|------------|-------------|----------------------|
| AG | AG01 | Farming | 6 |
|    | AG03 | Breeding | 8 |
|    | AG04 | Fishing | 1 |
| BU | BU01 | Management | 7 |
|    | BU02 | Operative | 47 |
|    | BU03 | Road making | 2 |
| MF | MF01 | Machinery | 17 |
|    | MF02 | Tools | 49 |
|    | MF03 | Shipbuilding | 4 |
|    | MF04 | Iron and steel | 28 |
|    | MF05 | Copper, tin and lead | 24 |
|    | MF06 | Gold, silver and jewels | 37 |
|    | MF07 | Earthenware | 33 |
|    | MF08 | Coal and gas | 1 |
|    | MF09 | Chemical | 19 |
|    | MF10 | Furs and leather | 23 |
|    | MF11 | Glue and tallow | 8 |
|    | MF12 | Hair | 14 |
|    | MF13 | Woodworkers | 44 |
|    | MF14 | Furniture | 55 |
|    | MF15 | Coaches | 46 |
|    | MF16 | Paper | 7 |
|    | MF17 | Floorcloth | 4 |
|    | MF18 | Woollens | 26 |
|    | MF19 | Cotton and silk | 9 |
|    | MF20 | Flax and hemp | 12 |
|    | MF21 | Lace | 23 |
|    | MF22 | Dyeing | 7 |
|    | MF23 | Dress | 53 |
|    | MF24 | Dress sundries | 33 |
|    | MF25 | Food preparation | 8 |

| Sector | Sub-sector | Description | Distinct occupations |
|---|---|---|---|
| | MF26 | Baking | 9 |
| | MF27 | Drink preparation | 13 |
| | MF28 | Smoking | 4 |
| | MF29 | Watches and instruments | 29 |
| | MF30 | Printing | 24 |
| | MF31 | Unspecified | 9 |
| TR | TR01 | Warehouses | 1 |
| | TR02 | Maritime navigation | 5 |
| | TR03 | Inland navigation | 8 |
| | TR05 | Roads | 30 |
| DE | DE01 | Coal | 20 |
| | DE02 | Raw materials | 66 |
| | DE03 | Clothing materials | 24 |
| | DE04 | Dress | 48 |
| | DE05 | Food | 85 |
| | DE06 | Tobacco | 4 |
| | DE07 | Wines, spirits and hotels | 39 |
| | DE08 | Coffee | 7 |
| | DE09 | Furniture | 14 |
| | DE10 | Stationery | 26 |
| | DE11 | Household utensils | 45 |
| | DE12 | General dealers | 38 |
| | DE13 | Unspecified | 28 |
| IS | IS01 | Accountants and clerks | 26 |
| | IS02 | Labourers | 1 |
| PP | PP01 | Central administration | 38 |
| | PP02 | Local administration | 29 |
| | PP04 | Army | 63 |
| | PP05 | Navy | 21 |
| | PP06 | Police and prisons | 8 |
| | PP07 | Law | 22 |
| | PP08 | Medicine | 27 |
| | PP09 | Graphic arts | 17 |
| | PP10 | Performing arts | 13 |
| | PP11 | Literature | 2 |
| | PP12 | Science | 1 |
| | PP13 | Education | 10 |
| | PP14 | Religion | 20 |

| Sector | Sub-sector | Description | Distinct occupations |
|--------|-----------|-------------|---------------------|
| DS | DS01 | Indoor service | 20 |
| | DS02 | Outdoor service | 66 |
| | DS03 | Other service | 24 |
| RE | RE00 | Miscellaneous status | 1 |
| | RE01 | Gentry | 1 |
| | RE02 | Esquires | 5 |
| | RE03 | Knights and baronets | 8 |
| | RE04 | Aristocracy | 10 |
| XX | XX00 | Unknown and missing | 1 |
| Total | | | 1,612 |

In detail, the following should be noted when the classification is applied to Westminster. Builders included those professionals connected with surveying and construction who might have been employers of labour; whilst the building operatives were included with those concerned with the construction of a property: bricklayers and masons, joiners and carpenters, slaters and tilers, painters and plumbers, plasterers and paperhangers. The finished products of this group were so fixed to the building that it became an integral part of it: thus joiners were held to be builders, whereas cabinet makers were held to be manufacturers of furnishings.

The allocation of occupations among the Manufacturers was more problematical than the allocation of occupations to that sector as a whole, revealing the central weakness of Booth's classification. Most occupations allocated to the Manufacturing sector contained the words 'maker', 'manufacturer', 'weaver', 'worker', 'wright', 'smith', or some other indication that the person was one who transformed raw materials by the application of skill, strength and energy to give them added value. It is arguable that some minor mis-classifications have occurred here; possibly the upholsterers and braziers should be placed among the Dealers.

The economic sector of Transport has also been stripped of some who might have been there: the coal heavers belong in the coal trade at DE01, and the warehousemen were placed in the dealing sector, their sub-sector being determined by the material they were wholesaling. This left in the Transport sector the wharfingers, the mariners, the inland waterways personnel, and those connected with road transport. This last was the most numerous group, including carmen, carters, draymen, waggoners, unspecified coachmen (although the coachman to Major Maine was a domestic servant), hackneymen, stable keepers, messengers and porters.

The economic sector of Dealing is a large and disparate one, but most in the sector used expressions such as 'dealer', 'merchant', 'vendor', 'factor', 'seller', 'shop', 'warehouse', 'chandler', '-monger' or the common suffix '-man'. This last was held to indicate a dealer, with the exception of such obvious anomalies as coachman and clergyman. The material being worked or dealt was also useful in allocating some occupations to economic sectors. Thus DE01 comprises the whole of the coal trade, including coal dealers, coalmen, coal merchants, coal chandlers, coal sellers, a 'coal shed', coal carmen, coal porters, coal heavers, coal meters and a coke merchant.

The Industrial Servants were few, including financial professionals – bankers, stockbrokers, insurance brokers, accountants and book keepers, and clerks of various descriptions. Generic labourers are also found here, following the example of Booth/Armstrong.

The sector of Public and Professional Service is large, although relatively easy to define. The army and navy personnel usually defined themselves clearly in their job descriptions, as did the legal and medical professions and the clergy. The sub-sectors for employees of central and local government were more difficult: the former include Members of Parliament, postmen, clerks to the War Office, and a messenger to the House of Commons, while the latter included lottery office keepers and lamplighters, the lessee of Covent Garden market, a clerk to the water works, and those responsible for the 'fire engine' at Pimlico. Another miscellany of occupations was to be found among the performing and creative artists: comedians, dancers and musicians; sculptors, historical engravers and Royal Academicians (although Sir Joshua Reynolds was described by his status, and George Frederick Handel was described as Esquire). Status designations were stripped from those who could be placed elsewhere: thus the Member of Parliament who was also a baronet would be found under PP01 (central administration) rather than RE03 (knights and baronets). This left a residuum who were classified in a broad hierarchy from the Free Denizen at RE00 to Irish peers and other members of the aristocracy at RE04. The largest groups in this sector were the gentlemen and esquires, who made up a major proportion of the voters, especially in St George.

The yeomen were an especially problematical group. Except in 1784, when nearly 200 yeomen polled, their numbers were generally small; they were classified amongst the soldiers in the belief that they were the royal bodyguard, the Yeomen of the Guard. But their voting did not resemble that of a royal bodyguard, and it is possible that the term indicated a status designation.

Domestic Service was a broad sector, although with the exception of hairdressers it included no numerically large groups. Indoor servants were distinguished from those outdoors such as coachmen, whilst the term 'gardener' was held to refer to market gardeners. The third group, called 'Domestic Service: Other', was as imprecise as the lack of a distinguishing characteristic suggests. They included hairdressers, rubbish collectors, bath house proprietors, firemen, chimney sweeps, cleaners of hats and pictures, laundrymen, and the bug destroyer.

Only four occupations remained unallocated, three of them because of difficulty in interpreting the contractions adopted by the poll clerks. The only unidentified occupation which sounds as if it means something was the solitary 'turnback', who thus joins the other oddities and missing values in the Unknown and Missing sector. The printed poll book of 1780 contained no occupations, although a few status designations were recorded in it, so the majority of these cases were also placed in the Unknown and Missing category.

Dual occupations presented problems of classification. The general rule was followed that the occupational description which conveyed most information took precedence. Thus the voter who described himself as a 'cordwainer and private soldier' was placed with the shoe makers (with a discrete code at the lowest level), whilst the army captain who took the style of 'gentleman' was placed with the military personnel. By the same token, the voter who described himself as a 'labourer and spruce beer maker' was placed with the drinks makers. Not all dual occupations were so easy. Others were classified under the first element, although with the qualification that the inverted order of the two occupations should receive the same code. Thus 'glazier and painter' received the same code as 'painter and glazier'. Most dual occupations were identically coded at the highest level; many, like the 'painter and glazier', were in the same second-level code. Few dual occupations came from wholly different economic sectors.

It is with the third level of the occupational classification that the Westminster Historical Database departs from the taxonomies of Booth and Armstrong. Whilst the original character strings of occupational descriptions are preserved, and the full eight-character code gives a unique code to each discrete occupation, the third level of the taxonomy aims to group related occupations. It must be admitted that the aim of giving related occupations a common seven-character code has been imperfectly achieved, and in any case disputes will persist as to what constitutes related occupations. But it is clear that grouping coal dealers and coal merchants together at DE01001 has added value for analytical purposes, since they can always be disaggregated at level 4 of the classification. Similarly, the capacity to distinguish between wine merchants (DE07001) on the one hand, and innkeepers, victuallers and publicans (DE07002) on the other, has added refinement and flexibility to the classification.

Further flexibility is provided by the many gaps in the classification which remain unfilled. Indeed, whilst the full classification consists of eight characters, no more that six of these are used. Given that the top level of the classification consists of only ten categories, it is not necessary to devote two characters to it. Moreover, the fifth character of the classification remains unused, which leaves potential for further ironing out of the wrinkles which remain. The third level of the classification is shown below in Table 4.8.

**Table 4.8 Level 3 occupational classification in the Westminster Historical Database**

| Code | Description |
|---|---|
| AG01001 | Chaffcutters |
| AG01002 | Farmers |
| AG01007 | Woodmen |
| AG01008 | Nurseymen |
| AG01009 | Gardeners |
| AG01013 | Husbandmen |
| AG03003 | Veterinary surgeons |
| AG03006 | Farriers |

| Code | Description |
|------|-------------|
| **AG03007** | Cow keepers |
| **AG04001** | Fishermen |
| **BU01001** | Architects |
| **BU01002** | Civil engineers |
| **BU01003** | Surveyors |
| **BU01005** | Builders |
| **BU01006** | Land surveyors |
| **BU02000** | Brick makers |
| **BU02001** | Masons |
| **BU02002** | Bricklayers |
| **BU02003** | Plasterers |
| **BU02004** | Slaters |
| **BU02006** | Carpenters, joiners |
| **BU02007** | Plumbers |
| **BU02008** | Painters |
| **BU02009** | Glaziers |
| **BU02010** | Paper hangers |
| **BU02014** | Stone masons |
| **BU02015** | Marble carvers |
| **BU02016** | Statuaries |
| **BU03001** | Paviours |
| **MF01001** | Engine makers |
| **MF01002** | Millwrights |
| **MF01003** | Engineers |
| **MF01004** | Pump makers |
| **MF01005** | Frame makers |
| **MF02000** | Curriers' tool makers |
| **MF02001** | Gun makers, gun smiths |
| **MF02002** | Letter founders |
| **MF02003** | Lock smiths |
| **MF02004** | Pencil makers |
| **MF02005** | Tool makers |
| **MF02006** | Cutlers, surgical instrument makers |
| **MF02007** | Blacking ball makers |
| **MF02008** | Cock founders |
| **MF02009** | Pin makers, needle makers |
| **MF02010** | Armourers |
| **MF02012** | Spring makers |
| **MF02013** | Sword cutlers |

| Code | Description |
|------|-------------|
| MF03001 | Boat builders |
| MF04000 | Iron plate makers |
| MF04001 | Iron founders |
| MF04002 | Drillers, grinders |
| MF04003 | Steel workers |
| MF04004 | Blacksmiths, smiths |
| MF04005 | Bed screw makers |
| MF04006 | Nailers |
| MF04008 | Wire workers, wire drawers |
| MF04009 | Plate case makers |
| MF05001 | Braziers, brass workers |
| MF05002 | Copper smiths |
| MF05003 | Lead pipe makers |
| MF05004 | Pewterers |
| MF05005 | Tin plate workers, tin men |
| MF05006 | Chasers |
| MF06000 | Silver chain makers |
| MF06001 | Silver smiths |
| MF06002 | Gold and silver workers |
| MF06003 | Goldsmiths |
| MF06004 | Jewellers |
| MF07001 | China makers, china painters |
| MF07002 | Glass cutters, glass painters |
| MF07003 | Enamellers, ornament makers, looking glass makers |
| MF07004 | Pipe makers |
| MF08001 | Gas lamp makers |
| MF09001 | Blue makers, blacking makers |
| MF09002 | Plaster makers |
| MF09003 | Starch makers |
| MF09004 | Colour makers |
| MF10001 | Curriers, leather dressers |
| MF10002 | Furriers |
| MF10003 | Holster makers |
| MF10004 | Bellows makers |
| MF11001 | Soap makers |
| MF12001 | Brush makers |
| MF12002 | Hair preparers, hair cloth weavers |
| MF12004 | Comb makers |
| MF12005 | Ivory turners |

| Code | Description |
|------|-------------|
| MF12006 | Whalebone cutters |
| MF13001 | Wood cutters |
| MF13002 | Printers' joiners |
| MF13003 | Coopers |
| MF13004 | Turners |
| MF13005 | Razor case makers |
| MF13006 | Cork cutters |
| MF13007 | Patten makers, pattern makers |
| MF13008 | Basket makers |
| MF13009 | Trunk makers |
| MF13010 | Case makers |
| MF13011 | Peg makers |
| MF13012 | Rocking horse makers |
| MF14000 | Writing case makers |
| MF14001 | Cabinet makers |
| MF14002 | Upholsterers |
| MF14003 | Carvers |
| MF14004 | Bedstead makers, mattress makers |
| MF14005 | Chair makers, chair carvers |
| MF14006 | Blind makers |
| MF14007 | Chimney piece makers |
| MF14008 | Billiard table makers |
| MF14009 | Furniture polishers |
| MF15000 | Coach merchants |
| MF15001 | Coach makers, coach smiths |
| MF15002 | Coach carvers, coach painters |
| MF15003 | Tyre smiths, wheelwrights |
| MF15004 | Bit makers, bridle makers, spur makers, stirrup makers |
| MF15005 | Saddle makers, saddle tree makers |
| MF16001 | Card makers |
| MF16002 | Paper makers |
| MF17001 | Floorcloth makers |
| MF18001 | Calenderers |
| MF18002 | Cloth workers |
| MF18003 | Felt makers |
| MF18004 | Framework knitters |
| MF18005 | Woolcombers |
| MF18006 | Weavers |
| MF19001 | Oil silk makers |

| Code | Description |
|------|-------------|
| MF19002 | Ribbon weavers |
| MF19003 | Silk weavers, plush weavers |
| MF19004 | Wadding makers |
| MF20001 | Linen weavers |
| MF20002 | Canvas makers |
| MF20003 | Flax spinners, flax dressers |
| MF20004 | Rope makers |
| MF21001 | Lace makers, embroiderers |
| MF21002 | Gold lace makers, gold thread makers, orris weavers |
| MF21003 | Artificial flower maker |
| MF21004 | Braid maker |
| MF22001 | Dyers, scourers |
| MF22002 | Calico glazers |
| MF22003 | Silk dyers |
| MF23001 | Tailors |
| MF23002 | Breeches makers |
| MF23003 | Hat makers, milliners |
| MF23004 | Shoe makers, boot makers, cordwainers |
| MF23005 | Army clothiers |
| MF23006 | Clog makers |
| MF23007 | Stay makers, stocking weavers |
| MF23008 | Habit makers, robe makers |
| MF24001 | Accountrement makers, peruke makers |
| MF24002 | Button makers |
| MF24003 | Buckle makers |
| MF24004 | Feather dressers, ostrich feather makers |
| MF24005 | Fan makers, stick makers, umbrella makers |
| MF25001 | Chocolate makers |
| MF25002 | Mustard makers |
| MF25003 | Millers |
| MF25004 | Sugar refiners |
| MF25005 | Vinegar makers |
| MF25006 | Macaroni makers |
| MF26001 | Bakers |
| MF26002 | Biscuit bakers, gingerbread bakers |
| MF26003 | Muffin makers, bun makers |
| MF26004 | Sweet makers |
| MF27001 | Brewers |
| MF27002 | Distillers |

| Code | Description |
|------|-------------|
| MF27003 | Soda water makers |
| MF27004 | Spruce beer makers |
| MF27005 | Malt makers |
| MF28001 | Tobacco makers |
| MF28003 | Snuff makers |
| MF29001 | Clock makers, watch makers |
| MF29002 | Musical instrument makers |
| MF29003 | Mathematical instrument makers |
| MF29004 | Fishing tackle makers |
| MF30001 | Printers |
| MF30002 | Copper plate printers |
| MF30003 | Book binders |
| MF30004 | Engravers |
| MF30005 | Music printers |
| MF30006 | Pocket book makers |
| MF30008 | Newspaper proprietors |
| MF31001 | Refiners |
| MF31002 | Miscellaneous makers |
| MF31003 | Miscellaneous manufacturers |
| TR01001 | Wharfingers |
| TR02001 | Mariners |
| TR02002 | Ship owners |
| TR03001 | Bargemen |
| TR03002 | Lightermen |
| TR03003 | Watermen |
| TR05001 | Carters, draymen, waggoners |
| TR05002 | Chairmen |
| TR05003 | Carmen |
| TR05004 | Hackney coachmen, coach masters |
| TR05005 | Stable keepers, ostlers |
| TR05006 | Porters |
| DE01001 | Coal dealers, coal men, coal merchants |
| DE01002 | Coal carters, coal heavers, coal meters, coal porters |
| DE02001 | Timber dealers |
| DE02002 | Hop dealers |
| DE02003 | Hay dealers |
| DE02004 | Corn merchants |
| DE02005 | Wool staplers, flax merchants |
| DE02006 | Sandmen |

| Code | Description |
|------|-------------|
| DE02007 | Salters, yeast merchants |
| DE02008 | Meal factors |
| DE02009 | Hair dealers |
| DE02010 | Malt dealers |
| DE02011 | Leather dealers |
| DE02013 | Ivory dealers, whalebone dealers |
| DE02014 | Diamond dealers |
| DE02015 | Marble dealers, stone dealers |
| DE02016 | Lime dealers |
| DE02017 | Cane dealers |
| DE02018 | Feather dealers |
| DE02019 | Wax chandlers, tallow chandlers, oilmen, colourmen |
| DE02020 | Lead dealers |
| DE02021 | Flour dealers |
| DE02022 | Blacking dealers, soot dealers |
| DE02023 | Bone merchants |
| DE02024 | Silver dealers, gold dealers |
| DE03001 | Rag dealers |
| DE03002 | Piece brokers |
| DE03003 | Cloth dealers, clothiers |
| DE03004 | Silk mercers |
| DE03005 | Lace dealers, linen drapers |
| DE03006 | Woollen drapers |
| DE03007 | Muslin dealers |
| DE03008 | Cotton dealers |
| DE04001 | Drapers |
| DE04002 | Hosiers |
| DE04003 | Hatters |
| DE04004 | Clothes dealers |
| DE04005 | Haberdashers |
| DE04006 | Mercers |
| DE04008 | Shoe dealers |
| DE04009 | Slopsellers |
| DE04010 | Button dealers, trimmings dealers |
| DE04011 | Glovers |
| DE04012 | Stick sellers, umbrella sellers |
| DE04013 | Blanket dealers, childbed linen warehouse keepers |
| DE04014 | Fancy warehouse keepers |
| DE05000 | Slaughtermen, horse flesh boilers, sheep's head dealers |

| Code | Description |
|---|---|
| DE05001 | Butchers, pork butchers, ham dealers, sausagemen |
| DE05002 | Poulterers |
| DE05003 | Fishmongers |
| DE05004 | Dairymen, milkmen |
| DE05005 | Cheesemongers |
| DE05006 | Coffee dealers, tea dealers |
| DE05007 | Grocers |
| DE05008 | Fruiterers, greengrocers |
| DE05009 | Potato dealers |
| DE05010 | Shellfish dealers, oyster dealers |
| DE05011 | Cook shop keepers |
| DE05012 | Tripe dealers |
| DE05013 | Pastrycooks |
| DE05014 | Butter dealers, egg dealers |
| DE05015 | Vinegar dealers |
| DE05016 | Herb dealers |
| DE05017 | Confectioners |
| DE05018 | Provision dealers |
| DE06001 | Tobacconists |
| DE06002 | Snuff dealers |
| DE07001 | Wine merchants |
| DE07002 | Innkeepers, victuallers, publicans, hotel keepers |
| DE07003 | Beer dealers |
| DE07004 | Cellarmen |
| DE07005 | Brandy dealers |
| DE07007 | Cider dealers |
| DE07008 | Spirit dealers |
| DE07011 | Liquor merchants |
| DE07012 | Water dealer, mineral water dealer, ginger beer dealer |
| DE08001 | Lodging house keepers |
| DE08002 | Coffee house keepers, eating house keepers |
| DE08003 | Waiters |
| DE09001 | Undertakers |
| DE09002 | Picture dealers |
| DE09003 | Pawnbrokers |
| DE09004 | Bedding warehousemen |
| DE09005 | Carpet warehousemen |
| DE09006 | Furniture warehousemen |
| DE09007 | Lampmen |

| Code | Description |
|------|-------------|
| DE09011 | Furniture brokers |
| DE10001 | Stationers, law stationers |
| DE10002 | Booksellers |
| DE10003 | News agents, news vendors |
| DE10004 | Music shop keepers, music sellers |
| DE10005 | Bill stickers |
| DE10006 | Map sellers, geographers |
| DE10007 | Print sellers |
| DE10008 | Paper sellers, paper warehousemen |
| DE10009 | Librarians, circulating librarians |
| DE11001 | Earthenware sellers, Staffordshire warehouse keepers |
| DE11002 | Glass sellers, glass dealers |
| DE11003 | China dealers |
| DE11004 | Ironmongers, hardware sellers, dealers in old iron |
| DE11005 | Bottle dealers |
| DE11006 | Mineralogists, dealers in curios |
| DE11007 | Turnery dealers |
| DE11008 | Lamp warehousemen |
| DE12001 | Chandlers |
| DE12002 | Sale shop keepers, junk dealers, shopkeepers |
| DE12003 | Florists |
| DE12004 | Hawkers |
| DE12005 | Medical warehouses, medicine sellers |
| DE12006 | Packers |
| DE12007 | Perfumers, lavender water sellers |
| DE12008 | Tool dealers, dealers in marine stores |
| DE12009 | Bird dealers, cow dealers |
| DE12010 | Toymen, Toyshopmen |
| DE13001 | Merchants |
| DE13002 | Agents, brokers, factors, travellers |
| DE13003 | Auctioneers, house agents, house brokers, appraisers |
| DE13004 | Warehousemen, foreign warehouse keepers |
| DE13005 | Birmingham agents |
| DE13006 | Nisu shop keepers |
| IS01001 | Bankers |
| IS01002 | Stock brokers |
| IS01003 | Insurance brokers |
| IS01004 | Accountants, book keepers |
| IS01005 | Draughtsmen |

| Code | Description |
|------|-------------|
| IS01006 | Livery company clerks |
| IS01007 | Clerks |
| IS01008 | Clerks |
| IS02001 | Labourers |
| PP01000 | Excisemen, measurers |
| PP01001 | MPs, Marshalsea court officers |
| PP01002 | Porters, postmen |
| PP01003 | Civil service clerks |
| PP01004 | Civil servants |
| PP01005 | Stationery office |
| PP01006 | Tidewaiters |
| PP02001 | Bailiffs, beadles, parish clerks, sextons, tomb showers |
| PP02002 | Water works employees, fire engine workers |
| PP02003 | Local government clerks |
| PP02004 | Inspectors |
| PP02005 | Lottery office keepers |
| PP02006 | Collectors |
| PP02007 | Market stewards |
| PP04001 | Colonels, lieutenant colonels |
| PP04002 | Generals, lieutenant generals |
| PP04003 | Major generals, majors |
| PP04004 | Captains |
| PP04005 | Army agents, Chelsea pensioners, lieutenants, yeomen |
| PP04006 | Other army officers |
| PP04007 | Sergeants |
| PP04008 | Corporals, army musicians |
| PP04009 | Soldiers, private soldiers |
| PP05001 | Admirals, vice admirals, rear admirals |
| PP05002 | Commanders |
| PP05003 | Captains RN, masters RN |
| PP05005 | Lieutenants RN |
| PP05006 | Royal Marines |
| PP05007 | Navy agents, navy officers |
| PP06001 | Constables, patrol men, Bow St officers, watchmen |
| PP07001 | Attorneys |
| PP07002 | Barristers |
| PP07003 | Solicitors |
| PP07004 | Serjeants at law |
| PP07005 | Scriveners |

| Code | Description |
| --- | --- |
| PP07006 | Conveyancers |
| PP07007 | Masters in Chancery |
| PP07008 | Doctors of law |
| PP07009 | Vice chancellors |
| PP08001 | Surgeons |
| PP08002 | Physicians, doctors, medical practitioners |
| PP08003 | Bleeders, cuppers |
| PP08004 | Dental surgeons |
| PP08005 | Oculists |
| PP08006 | Apothecaries, druggists, simplers, drug grinders |
| PP08007 | Chemists |
| PP08008 | Aurists |
| PP09001 | Artists, painters, portraitists, landscapists |
| PP09002 | Sculptors, figure casters |
| PP09003 | Heraldic painters |
| PP10001 | Composers, musicians, organists, Doctors of music |
| PP10002 | Comedians, dancers, stage proprietors |
| PP10003 | Tennis court keepers, fives court keepers |
| PP11001 | Writers |
| PP11002 | Shorthand writers |
| PP12001 | Mathematicians |
| PP13001 | Schoolmasters, teachers |
| PP13002 | Dancing-, riding-, fencing-, music-, writing-, drawing-masters |
| PP14000 | Curates |
| PP14001 | Clergymen |
| PP14002 | Ministers |
| PP14003 | Licensed preachers |
| DS01001 | Servants, butlers, cooks, stewards, valets |
| DS01002 | Footmen |
| DS01003 | Royal servants |
| DS02001 | Coachman |
| DS02003 | Gate keepers |
| DS03001 | Hairdressers |
| DS03002 | Dustmen, soil carriers, nightmen, rakers, scavengers |
| DS03004 | Bagnio keepers, bath house proprietors |
| DS03005 | Laundrymen, manglemen |
| DS03006 | Chimney sweeps, chimney doctors, bug destroyers |
| DS03007 | Glove cleaners, hat cleaners |

| Code | Description |
|------|-------------|
| **RE00001** | Free denizens |
| **RE01001** | Gentlemen |
| **RE02001** | Esquires |
| **RE03001** | Knights and baronets |
| **RE04001** | Rt Hons, peers |
| **XX00000** | Unclassified, missing |

The resulting overall classification for Westminster, while not perfect, showed that it could accommodate all occupations that were discovered in the poll books, and thus make the mass of data accessible for analysis. Moreover, it is a relatively straightforward matter for users to modify and adapt the occupational codes to analyse different constituencies using common codes. Since the original occupational strings still exist, as in the original poll book, this would involve taking one example of each occupation and creating a new look-up table containing both the occupations and the new codes. Such are the advantages of post-coding.

## 4.6 Conclusion

'Let a thousand flowers bloom' is likely to linger as the motto of socio-economic classification systems. Since the past is so diverse, the ways of approaching and interpreting it are likely also to remain diverse. That will prevent history as an academic discipline from becoming atrophied. 'Pluralism' should not, however, be allowed as an excuse for sloppy treatment of the data. As Kevin Schürer cogently argues, the requirements of aggregative analysis do not license the historian to forget the basic skills of historical analysis.[56] Thus sources and their deployment always require in-depth critical scrutiny. Rejection should still be the fate of all systems of classification that:

have major internal inconsistencies
appear historically implausible
involve changes to the original data, and/or
lack specification for fellow historians to check and validate both components and structure

Now that the problems are so well known and so well aired, it is a matter of common sense for historians to attend to 'best practice' when classifying historical occupations. In other words, a welcome diversity should continue – but not absolutely untrammelled.


*Notes*

1    The support of the ESRC for the research that has led to this assess-
     ment of occupations is gratefully acknowledged. For details, see proj-
     ect report P.J. Corfield, 'Urban occupations in Britain in the early
     industrial revolution' [ESRC FOO/23/2077: 1983-5]; and Green,
     'Thesis'. In addition, the authors thank Peter Clark and the late Her-
     man Diederiks for substantive discussions on occupational classifica-
     tion; the staff of Royal Holloway's Computer Centre for technical
     assistance over many years; and Tony Belton for practical advice and
     encouragement. A copy of P.J. Corfield's report upon 'Classifying
     Historical Occupations' is available from the ESRC Data Archive at
     the University of Essex, with the data on urban occupations in
     'Directories Database, 1772-87'.

2    Only Martineau's account of this meeting has survived: see H. Mar-
     tineau, *Autobiography*, ed. M.W. Chapman (1877), i, p. 398. For her
     own use of 'capital' and 'labour', see her *Illustrations of political
     economy* (1834), i, pp. xiv-xv.

3    In 1886 Charles Booth proposed that henceforth manufacturers and
     retailers should be differentiated in the census. Its coordinator Dr Ogle
     responded: 'The fact was the terms in which people returned them-
     selves to the census did not enable them to be distinguished in the way
     Mr. Booth suggested'. And Ogle cited the case of the hatter and the
     shoemaker. See C. Booth, 'Occupations of the people of the United
     Kingdom, 1801-81', *Journal of the [Royal] Statistical Society of
     London*, 49 (1886), pp. 314-444.

4    L.A. Clarkson, *The pre-industrial economy in England, 1500-1750*
     (1971) describes early modern England without reference to the con-
     cept ('capital' is indexed but not 'capitalism') and many neo-classical
     economic historians follow suit: see e.g. E.A. Wrigley, *Continuity,
     chance and change: the character of the industrial revolution in
     England* (Cambridge, 1988). Yet for I. Wallerstein, *Historical capital-
     ism* (1983), p. 19 and J. Vaizey, *Capitalism* (1971), p. 71 the late fif-
     teenth/sixteenth/seventeenth centuries are assumed to have seen the
     birth of a new economic system.

5    Examples cited in M.B. Katz, 'Occupational classification in history', *Journal of Interdisciplinary History*, 3 (1972/3), p. 70.

6    See e.g. M. Roberts, 'Women and work in sixteenth-century English towns' in Corfield and Keene (eds), *Work in towns*, pp. 86-102.

7    P.J. Corfield, 'Defining urban work', in ibid., p. 217. For the varieties of omissions and changing classification of what constituted 'work' in the censuses, see also J.M. Bellamy, 'Occupation statistics in the nineteenth-century censuses', in R. Lawton (ed.), *The census and the social structure: an interpretative guide to the nineteenth-century censuses for England and Wales* (1978), pp. 165-78.

8    O'Gorman, *Voters, patrons, and parties*, pp. 398-9.

9    Thus 'combing required a considerable measure of skill': H. Heaton, *The Yorkshire woollen and worsted industries from the earliest times up to the industrial revolution*, (Oxford, 1965), p. 263.

10    *O.E.D.* notes that the term could refer generally to an inventor or designer, as well as specifically to one who designed and constructed engines and public works.

11    R.A. Buchanan, *The engineers: a history of the engineering profession in Britain, 1750-1914* (1989), p. 11.

12    See *O.E.D.* for variant usages.

13    For an early survey of this material, see E.M. Green, 'The taxonomy of occupations in late eighteenth-century Westminster', in Corfield and Keene (eds), *Work in towns*, pp. 164-81.

14    Based on 5,028 cases from 1818, which have been linked between the poll books and rate books. Cases were linked by Standardised surname, Shortened forename, Parish and Street of residence.

15    For problems in incorporating wealth data into occupational classifications, see T. Hershberg and R. Dockhorn, 'Occupational classification', *Historical Methods Newsletter*, 9 (1975/6), pp. 59-60.

16    For an example of an exercise in flexible social cartography based upon occupational titles, that does not make any standard assumption about social 'levels', see M. Gribaudi and A. Mogoutov, 'Social stratification and complex systems: a model for the analysis of relational data' in K. Schürer and H. Diederiks (eds), *The use of occupations in historical analysis* (Göttingen: Max Planck Institut für Geschichte, 1993), pp. 53-74.

17    S.A. Royle, 'Aspects of nineteenth-century small town society: a comparative study from Leicestershire', *Midland History*, 5 (1979/80), pp. 50-62; with details of his social classification, pp. 60-1.

18    W.A. Armstrong, *Stability and change in an English county town: a social study of York, 1801-51* (1974), pp. 163-4. For a study that uses

a mixture of servant-keeping and occupational criteria to define an urban bourgeoisie, see also T. Koditshek, *Class formation and urban industrial society: Bradford, 1750-1850* (Cambridge, 1989), esp. pp. 585-9.

[19] See *inter alia* P. Earle, *The making of the English middle class: business, society and family life in London, 1660-1730* (1989) and J. Barry and C. Brooks (eds), *The middling sort of people: culure, society and politics, 1550-1800* (1994); and a growing volume of studies of nineteenth-century America, e.g. S.M. Blumin, *The emergence of the middle class: society and experience in the American city, 1760-1900* (Cambridge, 1989).

[20] For variants, see P.J. Corfield, 'Class by name and number in eighteenth-century Britain' in idem (ed.) *Language, history and class* (Oxford, 1991), esp. pp. 115-21.

[21] P. Colquhoun, *A treatise on the wealth, power and resources of the British empire* ... (1814), pp. 106-7.

[22] E.g. for an analysis that takes the 'fuzziness' of class for granted and which investigates overlapping and alternative bases for popular loyalties, see P. Joyce, *Visions of the people: industrial England and the condition of class, 1840-1914* (Cambridge, 1991), pp. 1-16, 332-42.

[23] W.A. Armstrong, 'The use of information about occupation, Part 1: a basis for social stratification', in E.A. Wrigley (ed.) *Nineteenth-century society: essays in the use of quantitative methods for the study of social data* (Cambridge, 1972), pp. 200-11.

[24] For the subjectivities at the heart of this classification, see esp. S.R.S. Szreter, 'The genesis of the Registrar-General's social classification of occupations', *British Journal of Sociology*, 35 (1984), pp. 522-46; and J.A. Banks, 'The social structure of nineteenth-century England as seen through the census', in Lawton (ed.), *The census and the social structure*, pp. 179-223.

[25] Armstrong, 'The use of information about occupation', in Wrigley (ed.), *Nineteenth-century society*, p. 424, n. 31.

[26] For data and criticisms, see ibid., pp. 212-14, incl. Table 3.

[27] D. and J. Mills, 'Occupation and social stratification revisited: the census enumerators' books in Victorian Britain', *Urban History Yearbook 1989* (1989), p. 63; with cross-references between directories and census, p. 68; and their amendments to Booth/Armstrong, pp. 73-5.

[28] G.A. Crossick, 'From gentleman to the residuum: languages of social description in Victorian Britain' in Corfield (ed.), *Language, history and class*, pp. 167-9.

29    P.J. Corfield, 'The Rivals: landed and other gentlemen', in N.B. Harte and R. Quinault (eds), *Land and society in Britain, 1700-1914: essays in honour of F.M.L. Thompson* (Manchester, 1996), pp. 1-30.

30    WAC Objections made by the counsel for Sir George Vandeput, Bt, on the poll for St Margaret and St John the Evangelist, Westminster, E/3078, fos 10 and 24.

31    All examples from the Westminster Historical Database.

32    No doubt for this reason, many write about social class without a strict occupational classification. For the problems, see also R.J. Morris, *Class, sect and party: the making of the British middle class: Leeds, 1820-50* (Manchester, 1990), esp. pp. 3, 8-14, 328-9.

33    Some examples of systems of 'prestige' allocation are listed in K. Mandemakers, 'Basic elements of a scheme for successful classification of occupational titles in an interdisciplinary, historical and international perspective' in Schürer and Diederiks (eds), *Use of occupations*, pp. 41-3; and earlier in 1977 D.J. Treiman suggested a pioneering international classification to show *Occupational prestige in comparative perspective* (New York, 1977).

34    For a sustained critique of modern social classifications based upon occupational data alone, see P. Doorn, 'Social structure and the labour market: occupational ladders, pyramids and onions' in Schürer and Diederiks (eds), *Use of occupations*, pp. 75-100. One study that *did* helpfully use additional information about income levels and employment status is M. Anderson, *Family structure in nineteenth-century Lancashire* (1971) but this study stands very much on its own.

35    The problems and prospects for the creation of a cross-national, cross-temporal historic-linguistic occupational machine-readable dictionary are noted by H.A. Diederiks and H.D. Tjalsma, 'The classification and coding of occupations in the past: some experiences and thoughts' in Schürer and Diederiks (eds), *Use of occupations*, pp. 29-30, 36-40; and by Mandemakers, 'Basic elements' in ibid., pp. 41-8.

36    R.J. Morris, 'Fuller values, questions and contexts: occupational coding and the historian' in ibid., p. 9.

37    The editors of urban directories usually collated their own data but also encouraged people to send corrections as well. For the ill-paid labours of a data collector in first Manchester and later Guildford, see J.D. Burn, *The autobiography of a beggar boy* (1855), pp. 174-5.

38    Examples of surviving English dialect terminology in eighteenth-century directories include the 'raff-fitter' [raff = timber] in Newcastle upon Tyne; the 'helier' [ = slater or tiler] in the Midlands; and the 'grutt-maker' [grutt = groats or oatmeal] in Bristol. In addition, there

was an extensive range of variant terminology in eighteenth-century Scotland, including the 'baxter' [baker], 'cordner' [cordwainer], 'flesher' [butcher], 'grieve' [bailiff], and 'room-setter' [lodging house keeper].

[39] Armstrong, 'Use of information about occupation', in Wrigley (ed.), *Nineteenth-century society*, pp. 194-5.

[40] In the debate on the census returns cited above [n.3], William Ogle, the Superintendent of Statistics, emphasised that the census relied upon people's self-specification which rarely sought to elaborate or to provide additional information. Instead, he found the masses in general 'uneducated and suspicious of every question put to them'.

[41] Armstrong, 'Use of information about occupation', in Wrigley (ed.), *Nineteenth-century society*, p. 195.

[42] For the problems involved in an exercise linking English and Dutch classifications, see Diederiks and Tjalsma, 'Classification and coding', in Schürer and Diederiks (eds) *Use of occupations*, pp. 29-40. The authors note especially (p. 35) that incautious linkages merely multiplied the problems already inherent within each national coding.

[43] Hatters were a prime example cited by Booth when he discussed this problem; see above [n. 3].

[44] Column A from D. Galenson, *White servitude in colonial America: an economic analysis* (Cambridge, 1981), p. 35; Column B from J. Ellis, 'A dynamic society: social relations in Newcastle upon Tyne, 1660-1760', in P. Clark (ed.), *The transformation of English provincial towns, 1660-1800* (1984), pp. 217-20.

[45] For examples of diverse usages, see J. Patten, 'Urban occupations in pre-industrial England', *Transactions of the Institute of British Geographers*, n.s., 2 (1977), pp. 296-313, esp. pp. 308-10.

[46] A recalculation of England's occupational statistics is offered in P.H. Lindert, 'English occupations, 1670-1811', *Journal of Economic History*, 40 (1980), pp. 685-712; but this has by no means laid the debates to rest.

[47] See Booth as cited above [fn. 3] and adaptation in W.A. Armstrong, 'The use of information about occupation, Part 2: an industrial classification, 1841-91', in Wrigley (ed.) *Nineteenth-century society*, pp. 226-310.

[48] Most historians compromise here to a minimal extent in that very obvious abbreviations and variant readings are grouped together; but not all follow that practice. Since there may be many variants, the degree of rigour that is applied to the third-level coding crucially affects the number of discrete occupational titles discovered by each histo-

rian. In other words, those who list 'mer.' and 'merchant' as two separate avocations will obviously generate a higher total of separate occupations that those who count them as one. For an advocate of recording all variants 'exactly as they appeared in the document', see R.J. Morris, 'Occupational coding: principles and examples', *Historical Social Research*, 15 (1990), p. 5.

49 An example of a project using a threefold coding for occupational classification based upon Booth/Armstrong is P.J. Corfield 'Urban occupations in Britain in the early industrial revolution', for which see above [n.1]. Its occupational classification (Updated Booth/Armstrong 1) is now superseded by the classification offered here (Updated Booth/Armstrong 2). The data from this project are now deposited at the ESRC Data Archive at Essex University as 'Directories Database, 1772-87'.

50 Armstrong, 'Use of information about occupation', in Wrigley (ed.), *Nineteenth-century society*, p. 250.

51 For a further discussion of the problematic status of gentlemen in the period, see Corfield, 'The Rivals: landed and other gentlemen', in Harte and Quinault (eds), *Land and society in Britain* pp. 1-33.

52 For detailed adaptation for the Westminster Historical Database, see following section 4.5.

53 Armstrong, 'Use of information about occupation', in Wrigley (ed.), *Nineteenth-century society*, pp. 229, 253.

54 This total includes the 'Unknown and Missing' values, and gives distinct codes (our error) for the Upholders and Upholsterers, which are synonymous.

55 Among this plethora of occupations is to be found at least one usage preceding that first recorded in *O.E.D.*, viz. 'cossack maker', a maker of high boots, in 1819 (first recorded English usage 1831).

56 K. Schürer, 'Understanding and coding occupations of the past: the experience of analysing the censuses of 1891-1921', in Schürer and Diederiks (eds), *Use of occupations*, pp. 107-8.

# 5

# Information Retrieval

There are two essential strategies for querying databases like the Westminster Historical Database. The first of these is to use Query by Example (QBE), in which search criteria are filled in on screen. The second is to use a query language, of which SQL, the Structured Query Language, is the international standard. Query languages are high-level languages which allow users to create and manipulate a database using English-like statements. Moreover, they are non-procedural: the user specifies what is to be done, rather than telling the system how to do it. As a standard language, SQL can be run on a variety of platforms from the mainframe to the micro. It should be noted that QBE is usually a front-end which conceals the operation of SQL behind the scenes.

Each of these strategies has its advantages and disadvantages. QBE has the advantage of simplicity, in that there is no need to learn a query language or its syntax. But these advantages quickly disappear with increasingly complex querying and with the addition of many limiting conditions to queries. For regular and intensive work, for more complex querying, and for the development of search and record linkage algorithms it is preferable to use a query language that will offer a high degree of refinement.

This chapter is dedicated to explaining querying using SQL. It is not a comprehensive guide, although it may be noted that there are plenty of these available.[1] Rather, the aim is to give a flavour for querying, together with specimen queries which should cover the needs of most users. These specimen queries will, of course, have to be adapted to suit the needs of the individual user.

## 5.1 A note for novices

Many users of the Westminster Historical Database will be seeking information about specific subjects. Some of them will be unfamiliar with database systems. This brief note is intended to help them undertake simple queries. It should suffice to get users started, although they will still need to read the summary of the fields and tables in the Database (Chapter 3), and they may well need to read more of this chapter. In the following sections, for ease of identification, computer commands and printout are in a `Courier` (monospaced) font. Additionally, the names of tables and entities are in **`Courier bold`**, whilst fieldnames are in *`Courier italic`* (though this would not be required in practice). It should, however, be remembered that querying could be case-sensitive, in which case all search criteria should be entered in upper-case characters.

A simple SQL query, which must be terminated with a semi-colon, follows the syntax:

`SELECT` some fields `FROM` a table `WHERE` a search criterion is fulfilled.

Thus:

```
SELECT Fname, Surname, Parish, Street, Occup, Vote
FROM P1749
WHERE Surname = 'HANDEL';
```

This will return the following record:

| FNAME | SURNAME | P | STREET | OCCUP | VOTE |
|---|---|---|---|---|---|
| GEORGE FREDERICK | HANDEL | C | BROOK ST | ESQ | 10 |

A simple query may return many records, depending on the search criterion. The search may be focused by specifying further search criteria which must be fulfilled. Searches are narrowed by adding the `AND` command, since the search must now satisfy all criteria. Thus:

```
SELECT Fname, Parish, Street, Occup, Vote
FROM P1749
WHERE Parish= 'F'
AND Occup= 'CARPENTER';
```

## 5.2 Selecting data

The most important and most frequently used SQL command is
SELECT, which is used to query data in the tables. Using SELECT
enables the user to carry out three essential database operations:

*Selection* retrieves all the records from a table that meet a
specified condition, such as Vote = '001'.

*Projection* extracts from all records only those fields which are
specified in the query. For example, a query specifying just the
Parish and Vote fields of the table **P1819** does not retrieve
or display the other fields in that table.

*Joining* involves combining two or more tables that contain
related data and have a common field or fields. The result of the
query may contain any of the fields present in the joined tables,
but only a single copy of the joined fields.

The SELECT command consists of up to six clauses, which must
always occur in the following sequence:

```
SELECT
FROM
WHERE
GROUP BY
HAVING
ORDER BY
```

### a) SELECT and FROM

Whilst the other four clauses are optional, SELECT and FROM are
a mandatory part of every query. The SELECT clause describes
which columns (fields) should be retrieved. The field names are
listed, separated by commas. The order in which they are given
determines how they are listed in the results table. The FROM
clause appears immediately after the SELECT clause, and defines
the table (or tables) that contain the columns specified in the
SELECT statement. Each query is terminated with a semi-colon.

At its simplest, then, a query involves just SELECT and FROM.
The following query will retrieve the contents of the fields *Fname*

and *Surname* for every record in the table **P1819** :

```
SELECT Fname, Surname
FROM P1819;
```

If, as often happens in a multitable database, there is a field with the same name in more than one table, the table name should be given just before the field name, and separated by a dot. The following query will retrieve the contents of the fields *Fname* and *Surname* for every record in the table **P1819**:

```
SELECT P1819.Fname, P1819.Surname
FROM P1819, P1820;
```

If all fields are to be retrieved, SELECT * can be used rather than laboriously typing in the name of each field. In this case, the sequence in which the field columns are displayed will depend upon the order in which they were created. The following query will retrieve the contents of all the fields of every record in the table **P1819**:

```
SELECT *
FROM P1819;
```

Alternatively, SELECT DISTINCT <*Fieldname*> can be used; in this case SQL will retrieve only those rows which are not duplicates. In some dialects of SQL this is performed by the command SELECT DISTINCTROW <*Fieldname*>. The following query will retrieve one example of every character string in the *Surname* field in the table **P1819**:

```
SELECT DISTINCT Surname
FROM P1819;
```

## b) The WHERE clause and types of search conditions

Using just the SELECT and FROM clauses, we can retrieve all the data in a table, or all the data in specified fields. However, in most cases we will want to refine our query to retrieve only those records (rows) which meet our particular search conditions. The WHERE clause is added immediately after the FROM clause, and is used to select those records which are of interest to us. The values held in each record are tested, and only those which satisfy the criteria following the WHERE clause are selected.

Since database querying is case sensitive, the character string sought must be entered in capitals as lower case characters are not used in the Westminster Database. Moreover, it should be noted that character strings as search criteria are enclosed within single quotation marks. This includes the *Vote* codes, which are characters rather than numbers. We may wish to know more about the economist David Ricardo by implementing the following query:

```
SELECT Fname, Surname, Parish, Street,
Occup, Vote
FROM P1819
WHERE Surname = 'RICARDO';
```

This will return the following record:

| FNAME | SURNAME | P | STREET | OCCUP | VOTE |
|-------|---------|---|--------|-------|------|
| DAVID | RICARDO | C | BROOK ST | ESQ | 100 |

More complex SQL queries can be built by having multiple search conditions. Search conditions can be combined together in a single WHERE clause using the logical operators AND, OR, NOT. It should be remembered that Boolean operators are counterintuitive. Use of the AND operator narrows the search, since only records which satisfy *all* of many search criteria are selected; use of the OR operator widens the search, since all records which satisfy *any* of many search criteria are selected. SQL provides five different types of search conditions: *comparison tests*, *range tests*, *set membership tests*, *pattern matching tests*, and *null value tests*. Comparison tests use the usual relational operators:

| Operator | Meaning | Operator | Meaning |
|----------|---------|----------|---------|
| = | Equal to | <= | Less than or equal to |
| < | Less than | >= | Greater than or equal to |
| > | Greater than | != | Not equal to |

In addition to comparing a field to a constant value, it is possible to compare the value of one field against another, provided that both fields are of the same type. The following query will select the all the contents of each field of every record from **R1818** from St Anne's parish where the value in the field *Rv* is 20 or more:

```
SELECT *
FROM R1818
WHERE Parish = 'A'
AND Rv >= 20;
```

It is also possible to specify range criteria. One way of range testing is to use AND. The following query would return all the contents of each field of every record from **R1818** from St Anne's parish where the value in the field *Rv* is at least 20 and no greater than 29:

```
SELECT *
FROM R1818
WHERE Parish = 'A'
AND Rv <= 20
AND Rv >= 29;
```

But this can quickly become tedious to type in, especially if several sets of criteria are needed. Range comparisons can be simplified by using BETWEEN. Note that BETWEEN is inclusive meaning <= and >=.

```
SELECT *
FROM R1818
WHERE Rv BETWEEN 20 AND 29;
```

Alternatively, the BETWEEN command can be negated by the NOT operator:

```
SELECT *
FROM R1818
WHERE Rv NOT BETWEEN 20 AND 29;
```

Set membership records are used when we wish to retrieve records where a particular field contains certain specified values. This could be done by using the WHERE clause, together with the OR operator.

```
SELECT *
FROM P1819
WHERE Street = 'OXFORD ST'
OR Street = 'PICCADILLY'
OR Street = 'STRAND';
```

Again, this would quickly become tedious if we were looking for more than a very few values. A better alternative is to use the IN operator:

```
SELECT *
FROM P1819
WHERE Street IN ('OXFORD ST', 'PICCADILLY',
'STRAND');
```

Like BETWEEN, the IN operator can be negated by NOT:

```
SELECT *
FROM P1819
WHERE Street NOT IN ('OXFORD ST',
'PICCADILLY', 'STRAND');
```

Pattern-matching is a very common type of querying. It is often desirable to retrieve records which fit a particular pattern. For pattern matching, SQL uses an underscore _ to match any one character, and the percent sign % to match any number of characters (including zero). These are equivalent to the ? and * wildcards in MSDOS, and are used in conjunction with LIKE and NOT LIKE. For example, they may be used to group words that commence in the same way, but are not identical. The following query will retrieve not just information relating to Ricardo, but also information relating to voters with surnames beginning 'RIC', such as Rice, Richardson and Rickards:

```
SELECT *
FROM P1819
WHERE Surname LIKE 'RIC%';
```

This is an example of truncation. Additionally, pattern matching can be used in reverse truncation, to match words with different prefixes. So a query to retrieve records relating to those voters who lived in Westminster's squares, as opposed to the inhabitants of roads, streets, lanes and courts, might contain the clause WHERE Street LIKE '%SQ'. It can also be used for midstring searching, to find words or phrases containing a particular string of characters, but with varying prefixes and suffixes.

Finally, SQL provides a facility for null testing. Nulls are quite distinct from zeroes or spaces, and are used to show where data are not known or not applicable. A typical example of this concerns the Occup field for much of P1780. To select records where a specified field contains a null value, the IS NULL clause is used:

```
SELECT *
FROM P1819
WHERE Fname IS NULL;
```

This would retrieve Dr Donahoo's [Donoughue's] record:

| FNAME | SURNAME | P | STREET | OCCUP | VOTE |
|-------|---------|---|--------|-------|------|
| | DONAHOO | F | ADAM ST | MD | 001 |

### c) Statistical functions and the GROUP BY clause

Arithmetic expressions can be included in SQL queries to perform calculations on numerical data. The usual arithmetic operators are used.

| Operator | Meaning |
|----------|---------|
| + | Plus |
| − | Minus |
| * | Multiply by |
| / | Divide by |

For example:

```
SELECT Rv + 20
FROM R1818;
```

would add 20 to the value stored in the $Rv$ field of each record in
**R1818**. Additionally, arithmetic expressions can be used to
compare the contents of one field with another. Also available are
the functions GREATEST, LEAST, ROUND and TRUNC.

The arithmetic expressions described above work on individual
records. However, the researcher often needs to obtain summary
data rather than voluminous printouts of every record that meets
the specified search criteria, and SQL incorporates a number of
statistical functions which work on columns of data. These column
functions are SUM, AVG, MIN, MAX, STDDEV, VARIANCE and
COUNT. FROM and WHERE can be employed in the usual way in
such queries to provide a good deal of flexibility. The following
query calculates and displays the minimum, maximum and average
(mean) rateable values in the table **R1818**:

```
SELECT MIN(Rv), MAX(Rv), AVG(Rv)
FROM R1818;
```

More complex querying will display more refined information. The
minimum, maximum, and average rateable values in St Anne's
parish in **R1818** may be displayed together with the range of
values by implementing the following query:

```
SELECT MIN(Rv), MAX(Rv), AVG(Rv),
MAX(Rv) - MIN(Rv)
FROM R1818
WHERE Parish = 'A';
```

The COUNT function is a special type of statistical function;
unlike the others its use is not confined to the numerical fields. It
may thus be used for many purposes in querying the Westminster
Database. If we wished to know how many records are to be found
in the table **P1819**, we could confirm this to be 6,556 by
implementing the query:

```
SELECT COUNT(*)
FROM P1819;
```

Or if we wished to know how many carpenters from St Martin's parish in 1819 appear in the Database, implementing the following query would show the number to be 37:

```
SELECT COUNT(*)
FROM P1819
WHERE Parish = 'F'
AND Oclv4 = 'BU020060';
```

This last criterion is preferable to the clause AND Occup = 'CARPENTER' since it will include typographical errors entered in the Database in the Occup field. The occupational code for CARPENTER is retrieved by implementing the query:

```
SELECT Oclv4
FROM DICTIONARY
WHERE Occup = 'CARPENTER';
```

The COUNT function is often combined with DISTINCT to ensure that identical entries are only counted once. For example, if we wanted to know how many different occupations were represented among the voters in 1819, we would be able to use the query:

```
SELECT COUNT(DISTINCT Occup)
FROM P1819;
```

If we omitted DISTINCT, COUNT would return a wrong answer, because many occupations were represented by more than one voter. If, however, we wished to record the frequency of occurrence of each occupation, we would implement the query:

```
SELECT Occup, COUNT(*)
FROM P1819
GROUP BY Occup;
```

## d) The HAVING clause

Sometimes, after using the GROUP BY clause, we may not wish to display all the groups created. For instance, we may wish to ignore any groups which only occur once. The HAVING clause may be used to remove groups of data in which we are not interested. Its function is like that of the WHERE clause, but whilst WHERE operates on rows of data (records), the HAVING clause works on groups of data. It compares a specified property of the group against a constant value. To continue the previous example:

```
SELECT Oclv4, Occup, COUNT(*)
FROM P1819
GROUP BY Oclv4, Occup
HAVING COUNT(*)>100;
```

This will select only those occupations represented by 100 or more voters in **P1819**, and will ignore those occupations represented by fewer than 100 voters:

| OCLV4 | OCCUP | COUNT(*) |
|---|---|---|
| BU020060 | CARPENTER | 204 |
| DE050010 | BUTCHER | 151 |
| DE070024 | VICTUALLER | 401 |
| MF230010 | SHOE MKR | 145 |
| MF260010 | BAKER | 133 |
| RE010010 | GENT | 622 |
| RE020010 | ESQ | 155 |

## e) The ORDER BY clause

Given the size of the Westminster Database, the output generated by a query can easily become unmanageable. Moreover, records will be displayed more or less at random, which is rarely of much use to the researcher. One way of making output more intelligible is to use the ORDER BY clause, which allows output to be displayed or printed in the order selected. It is always the last clause in a SELECT command. If many rows have identical values for a selected field, it will be necessary to select a secondary, and

perhaps a tertiary, sort field. Their names can be listed after ORDER
BY, separated by commas and with the primary sort field coming
first. If the user of the Westminster Database wished to audit the
accuracy of data entry, it would be useful to retrieve records in the
same order as they appeared in the original poll books and in which
they were entered. In the following example, records will be sorted
alphabetically by parish, and then in order of entry:

```
SELECT *
FROM P1819
ORDER BY Parish, Lineno;
```

## f) Joining tables

Until now, the queries which have been discussed have all been
based on a single table. However, a powerful feature of RDBMSs
is the ability to join multiple tables and retrieve the combined
information as a single list. In order to join two tables, there must
be at least one key field in the first table that has common data
values with a key field in the second table. Using SQL to retrieve
data from more than one table is a relatively simple task. First, each
table is named in the FROM clause, separated by a comma.
Secondly, the WHERE clause is used to make the connection and
compare fields in the different tables. For many purposes joining a
pair of tables will suffice; however, joins can be made just as easily
on three or more tables. Virtually any fields can be joined, provided
that they are of the same type and length.

To demonstrate the use of joins, we can query the tables P1819
and R1818 from the Westminster Historical Database. To begin,
we recall their structure using the DESCRIBE command:

```
DESCRIBE P1819;
```

| NAME | NULL? | TYPE |
|------|-------|------|
| PARISH | | VARCHAR2(1) |
| SURNAME | | VARCHAR2(40) |
| FNAME | | VARCHAR2(25) |
| STDSUR | | VARCHAR2(35) |
| SHTNAME | | VARCHAR2(4) |

```
STREET                    VARCHAR2(40)
OCCUP                     VARCHAR2(30)
OCLV4                     VARCHAR2(8)
OCLV3                     VARCHAR2(7)
OCLV2                     VARCHAR2(4)
OCLV1                     VARCHAR2(2)
VOTE                      VARCHAR2(6)
LINENO                    NUMBER(6)
SCODE                     VARCHAR2(5)
```

DESCRIBE **R1818**;

| NAME | NULL? | TYPE |
|------|-------|------|
| PARISH | | VARCHAR2(1) |
| WARD | | VARCHAR2(1) |
| SURNAME | | VARCHAR2(40) |
| FNAME | | VARCHAR2(25) |
| STDSUR | | VARCHAR2(35) |
| SHTNAME | | VARCHAR2(4) |
| STREET | | VARCHAR2(40) |
| LINENO | | NUMBER(6) |
| RV | | NUMBER(3) |
| SCODE | | VARCHAR2(5) |

Let us assume that we wished to retrieve data about the rateable values of houses inhabited by voters who lived in Soho Square in St Anne's parish. A join will have to be used because this information is not available from a single table. Rateable values are held in the *Rv* field of **R1818**, whilst the names of voters are held in the *Surname* field of **P1819**. Names of householders are held in the *Surname* field of **R1818**, which is thus the common field used to link data from the two tables.

```
SELECT P1819.Surname, P1819.Shtname,
P1819.Parish, P1819.Street, P1819.Occup,
R1818.Rv
FROM P1819, R1818
WHERE P1819.Parish = 'A'
AND R1818.Parish = 'A'
AND P1819.Street = 'SOHO SQ'
```

AND **R1818**.*Street* = 'SOHO SQ'
AND **P1819**.*Surname* = **R1818**.*Surname;*

The first four lines of the WHERE clause specify the criteria for selection. The last line uses the *Surname* field to make the join. Since fields in the different tables have the same name, then the table names must also be specified in the SELECT and WHERE clauses, as shown. If the asterisk had been used after SELECT, then much redundant data would have been retrieved. Consequently we would normally specify only the required fields when making multi-table joins.

It will be noted that apparently redundant search criteria have been included so that data are only retrieved for voters living in Soho Square in St Anne's parish. The reason for this is not simply that otherwise the resulting table would have required the publication of a second volume, but also because the voters and householders recorded in **P1819** and **R1818** as living in Soho Square happen to be list-unique in the *Surname* field in each table. If that were not the case, that is, if there had been more than one record in **P1819** or **R1818** with the same value in the field *Surname*, then we would have had to create temporary tables containing list-unique subsets of the data before linking from these to the poll and rate tables containing the data sought. This is discussed in greater detail in Chapter 6 below. Nevertheless, on implementing the simplified query, the following records are returned:

| Surname | Shtname | P | Street | Occup | Rv |
|---------|---------|---|--------|-------|----|
| ARROWSMITH | AARO | A | SOHO SQ | GEOGRAPHER | 125 |
| BAIKIE | JAME | A | SOHO SQ | GENT | 100 |
| BELL | CHAR | A | SOHO SQ | SURGEON | 172 |
| CURTIS | JOHN | A | SOHO SQ | SURGEON | 100 |
| KNIGHT | RICH | A | SOHO SQ | MP | 100 |
| MARSHALL | JOHN | A | SOHO SQ | UPHOLSTERER | 150 |
| YARNOLD | WILL | A | SOHO SQ | COAL MERCHANT | 70 |

The example given above is an *equi-join*; that is to say, the join condition includes the equals sign. It is also possible to make joins which do not include the equals sign. These are called *non-equi-joins* or *theta-joins*, and can use any of the following operators:

!=, <, >, <=, >=, BETWEEN and LIKE. The following query retrieves data about voters living in Soho Square who gave different occupational descriptions in successive elections. It is a legal query because **P1819**.*Surname* and **P1820**.*Surname* are the same type and length of field.

```
SELECT P1819.Surname, P1819.Shtname,
P1819.Parish, P1819.Street, P1819.Occup,
P1820.Occup
FROM P1819, P1820
WHERE P1819.Parish = 'A'
AND P1820.Parish = 'A'
AND P1819.Street = 'SOHO SQ'
AND P1820.Street = 'SOHO SQ'
AND P1819.Surname = P1820.Surname
AND P1819.Occup != P1820.Occup;
```

The following records will be retrieved:

| Surname | Shtname | P | Street | P1819.Occup | P1820.Occup |
|---------|---------|---|--------|-------------|-------------|
| CURTIS | JOHN | A | SOHO SQ | SURGEON | AURIST |
| KNIGHT | RICH | A | SOHO SQ | MP | GENT |

## g) Stored queries

Especially when two or more tables are to be joined, typing in queries can become very time-consuming. Fortunately, queries can easily be saved to a disk file for future use. Stored queries provide a convenient way of entering complex queries without typing them in anew each time they are used. When the filename is specified, the database management system looks up the query stored in the file, and executes it. The command SAVE <filename> will save the query to disk with the specified name. If no suffix is given, the default suffix .SQL will be used. For example:

SAVE **P19_20JOBS.SQL**

The command GET <filename> will return and display the query contained in the GET statement. However, it will not immediately run the query. To run it, we then need to enter r (which will redisplay the query and run it) or / (which will run it without displaying the query). For example:

```
GET P19_20JOBS.SQL
/
```

As a quicker alternative to using the GET command, we could use @ <filename>, which will recall and run the query without displaying it.

```
@ P19_20JOBS.SQL
```

Stored queries can also be used to speed up the processing of a series of similar but not identical queries. Since the query file is a simple ASCII text file, it can easily be modified with a wordprocessor or screen editor. We will briefly run through the keystrokes used in the process of saving, retrieving, amending, and saving a query:

```
SELECT COUNT(*)
FROM P1819
WHERE Parish = 'A';

SAVE P1819A.SQL

GET P1819A.SQL

C/'A'/'B'

R

SAVE P1819B.SQL
```

## h) Views

An extension of the stored query concept is the *view*. SQL allows the creation of alternative views, or ways of looking at the data. Put simply, a view is a window which restricts the viewer's attention to a selected portion of the underlying data. More formally, a view 'can be considered as a set of instructions to the RDBMS how to extract the required information from the defined tables which constitute the source of the data'.[2] Thus views are *virtual tables* – collections of data which have no independent existence, but which are derived from one or more real tables. If the underlying tables are erased, the view is destroyed as well. In general, though they contain no data of their own, views can be operated on and modified just as though they were real tables.

Views have a number of advantages and uses: most importantly, they simplify data access. Views can be used as filters in order to look at a subset of the data. Alternatively, they may be used to join two or more tables which will frequently be linked. Even if in fact a view is a multitable query, it looks like a single table to the user and can be manipulated as such, reducing keystrokes and errors. This is of particular benefit if the database user is inexperienced and likely to be confused by the need to join two or more tables.

It must be repeated, however, that the result is a virtual table, not a real one. Each time the view is accessed, the query will be run *ab initio*. This has both advantages and drawbacks. The principal benefit is that if the base tables are updated, the next time they are accessed through the view the updated data will automatically be used. The principal drawback is that using views can be very slow; it might appear to the user that a single table is being used, but behind the scenes there may well be a very complex multitable join which is rerun each time the view is used. It is for this reason that users wishing to perform wholesale record linkage exercises may prefer the strategy of creating temporary tables to hold subsets of the data, for example, those records which are common to two or more tables and list unique in each. Strategies using temporary tables are outlined below, and they are discussed in greater detail in Chapter 6.

Defining and using views are straightforward tasks. The CREATE VIEW command is used to name the view and describe, in the form of a SQL query, what the view is to contain. The following command is used to create a view called **Coaches**, which might be used to find out more about those engaged in the coach-making trades. It contains the five fields *Fname, Surname, Parish, Street, Occup, Oclv4*, and *Vote*.

```
CREATE VIEW COACHES AS
SELECT Fname, Surname, Parish, Street,
Occup, Oclv4, Vote
FROM P1819
WHERE Oclv2 = 'MF15';
```

To find out more about some of these coach makers, we could then
query the **COACHES** view rather than the entire table **P1819**:

```
SELECT *
FROM COACHES
WHERE Street = 'LONG ACRE';
```

## i) Temporary tables

The tables found in the Westminster Historical Database may not
be sufficient for all purposes. From time to time users may wish to
create temporary tables to hold a subset of the data contained in
the data tables. In particular, temporary tables offer a useful short-
cut to increase the speed of implementation of record linkage
queries. For example, users working on the election of 1818 may
frequently wish to find the rateable values of property occupied by
voters in that year. Many of those voters will have been list-unique
in both the poll and rate books at the level of *Surname*, *Stdsur*,
*Parish* and *Street*. Creating a temporary table of those who
were common to **P1818** and **R1818** would involve the following
three queries:

```
CREATE TABLE P1818TEMPA
AS SELECT Surname, Shtname, Parish, Street
FROM P1818
GROUP BY Surname, Shtname, Parish, Street
HAVING COUNT(*)=1;
```

```
CREATE TABLE R1818TEMPA
AS SELECT Surname, Shtname, Parish, Street
FROM R1818
GROUP BY Surname, Shtname, Parish, Street
HAVING COUNT(*)=1;
```

```
CREATE TABLE PR1818TEMPA
AS SELECT P1818TEMPA.Surname,
P1818TEMPA.Shtname, P1818TEMPA.Parish,
P1818TEMPA.Street
FROM P1818TEMPA, R1818TEMPA
WHERE P1818TEMPA.Surname=R1818TEMPA.Surname
AND P1818TEMPA.Shtname=R1818TEMPA.Shtname
AND P1818TEMPA.Parish=R1818TEMPA.Parish
AND P1818TEMPA.Street=R1818TEMPA.Street;
```

The records in **P1818** and **R1818** may then be linked using the temporary table **PR1818TEMPA**, as described in Chapter 6.


## 5.3 Displaying and printing the data

The ability to produce printed reports incorporating the results of queries is fundamental to any information management system. The task of describing the format and layout of the report is known as the *report definition*. The two main ways of presenting the results of a query are one record at a time (i.e. all the data relating to a record on a single page) or with many records in a tabular format. One record at a time is useful for such tasks as checking data entry for typing errors or reading long text fields, but for most purposes a tabular format is preferable. A report generator is used to group the output with subtotals and other summary statistics, and provided with headings and page numbers.

As with any other database-related activity, report generation benefits from careful planning; the task is both to ensure that the right data are retrieved, and that they are presented in a clear and unambiguous way, so that the reader can readily appreciate the significance of the results. The essential steps are:

Select the input file (table) containing the data
Identify fields to be included in the report
Determine the selection criteria which determine the records to be selected
Add any level breaks and group summaries required
Define layout – headers and footers, pagination, etc.

Save the query
Test output

The following example draws upon the Westminster Historical Database to demonstrate the preparation of a report. It is based upon Oracle and SQL*Plus. For our report, we wish to list all the rateable values in the table **R1818**, grouped by parish, ward and street. We also want to calculate and print the average rateable value in each street within each parish.

Having established that all the necessary information is held in the table **R1818**, the first stage is to specify the fields to be printed in the report, together with any selection criteria which may be required. This is done by a standard SQL query statement:

```
SELECT Parish, Ward, Street, Rv
FROM R1818
ORDER BY Parish, Ward, Street;
```

## a) The BREAK and COMPUTE commands

Having selected the data and the sequence in which it will appear, we can begin to format the report. First, we want to create blocks of data so that they are easily identifiable, and comparisons can readily be made between them. The BREAK command identifies a group of data with a common property. In our example, we want to group all records relating to a particular parish, and therefore break on the *Parish* field. We then want to sub-group by *Ward*, and then by *Street*. Finally, we want to insert a blank line (SKIP 1) between the groups. The complete command is:

```
BREAK ON Parish ON Ward ON Street SKIP 1;
```

The use of breaks will enable two activities to be carried out. First, the block itself can be clearly identified to the reader by means of the space separating it from the next group. Second, arithmetic group summary functions can now be applied to members of the group. In this case, we want to calculate the average rateable value (*Rv*) of property in each *Street*. This is done with the COMPUTE command, which enables the group summary functions described earlier – AVG, SUM, STD, MAXIMUM, MINIMUM, STDDEV, VARIANCE, COUNT – to be applied to groups of records generated with the BREAK command. The COMPUTE command is thus dependent upon the BREAK command, without which group summary functions cannot occur. The command we require is:

COMPUTE AVG OF *Rv* ON *Street*;

This will ensure that for each street the average rateable value will be printed in the *Rv* column.


## b) The COLUMN commands

Having specified the required breaks and group summaries, we can now turn to improving the readability of our printout by adding column headings. Strictly speaking, it is not necessary to specify the headings for each column (field) in the report; as a default, the fieldnames will be used. However, it is often a good idea to choose alternative headings which help to clarify the function of the columns, especially if abbreviations were used when naming the fields. This can be done using the COLUMN HEADING command: the syntax is COLUMN <fieldname> HEADING <'column title'>.

COLUMN *Rv* HEADING 'Rateable|Value'

Rateable Value is spelled out in full, rather than being abbreviated like the equivalent fieldnames. It is, however, a long column heading, and the vertical bar ensures that it will be displayed on two lines rather than one.

Readability will also be enhanced by adjusting the column spacing. There are various ways to adjust the width of fields and spacing between them. SET commands affect default values; often, though, we will want to control the width of individual columns rather than assigning a particular default value. Let us assume that in our sample report definition we do not wish to alter the default values; however, we wish to reduce the width of the Street column to 25 alphanumeric characters, cut the maximum size of the Parish column to 6 characters, cut the size of the Ward column to 4 characters, and set the size of the Rv column at 3 characters. This can be achieved with the COLUMN FORMAT command. As can be seen below, the way this is done depends upon the type of data:

```
COLUMN Street FORMAT A25
COLUMN Parish FORMAT A6
COLUMN Ward FORMAT A4
COLUMN Rv FORMAT 999
```

## c) The complete report definition

The report definition is now complete, and reads as follows:

```
BREAK ON Parish ON Ward ON Street SKIP 1
COMPUTE AVG OF Rv ON Street
COLUMN Parish HEADING 'Parish' FORMAT A6
COLUMN Ward HEADING 'Ward' FORMAT A4
COLUMN Street HEADING 'Street' FORMAT A26
COLUMN Rv HEADING 'Rateable|Value' FORMAT
999

SELECT Parish, Ward, Street, Rv
FROM R1818
ORDER BY Parish, Ward, Street;
```

Once the disk file containing the finished report definition has been created, the user can send the report to the printer, by specifying the output port and printer to be used, and typing:

```
SPOOL <filename>
RUN;
```

Spooling is ended with the command:

```
SPOOL OFF;
```

A sample from the resulting report is provided in Fig. 5.1.

## Figure 5.1 Sample printout of the completed report

```
                                          RATEABLE
PARISH WARD STREET                        VALUE
------ ---- ------------------------      --------
A      A    ALLENS CT                            8
                                                 8
                                                 8
            ***********************      --------
            avg                                  8

            BATEMANS BLDGS                      30
                                                30
                                                30
                                                30
                                                32
                                                32
                                                32
                                                32
                                                28
                                                30
                                                30
                                                32
                                                32
                                                30
                                                32
                                                32
            ***********************      --------
            avg                             30.875
```

This chapter has summarised the key features which make SQL powerful and easy to use. There are many more features, though most of them will rarely be needed by most database user. In particular, relatively little has been said about the arithmetic commands available within SQL. There are two reasons for this omission. First, the only numeric data in the Westminster Historical Database is contained in the field $Rv$. Secondly, the ability to spool output to a named file opens up the possibility of more complex data analysis using SPSS or a similar statistical package. Even a relatively simple statistical package such as MINITAB is far more sophisticated than the functions available within SQL, and experienced users in universities and elsewhere may well wish to export data from the Database for further analysis using a statistical package with which they are familiar.

The advantages of using SQL for information retrieval should be obvious. In the first place, it encourages precision. One of the principal characteristics of SQL is that the user does not have to know where data items are stored in order to retrieve them. However, the user must have a good understanding of the data and know the structure of the database if it is to be queried properly. SQL encourages – indeed requires – precision in the formulation of queries. Secondly, search algorithms of any level of complexity can be implemented. The most involved algorithms can be tested and refined in a progressive manner, and the resulting queries saved to disk for future use.

The following chapter will take information retrieval a stage further through an exploration of the theory and practice of record linkage in historical research. This involves the retrieval of information relating to an individual entity (probably but not necessarily a person) from two or more database tables.

*Notes*

[1]      See, for example, G. Koch and K. Loney, *Oracle, the complete reference* (3rd edn, Berkeley, Ca., 1995).

[2]      M. Bronzite, *Introduction to Oracle* (Maidenhead, 1989), p. 141.

# 6

# Record Linkage

Record linkage is fundamental to the process of historical research. Whether historians are concerned with the history of a ship, a college, a regiment, a corporation or an individual, record linkage is integral to their research strategies. And yet few focus explicitly on the methodology of record linkage. Whilst the contents of a college's muniment room may *ipso facto* be related to that institution, historians frequently use information drawn from many discrete sources. But this may present problems as ships, towns, people and even colleges are not uniquely identified by name alone.[1]

The lack of unique identification may be easily overcome in the case of famous institutions or individuals. Trinity College, Cambridge, is not confused with those in Oxford and Dublin; William Morris, the designer and socialist, is not confused with the eponymous motor car manufacturer; and Beatrice Webb, *née* Potter, did not write about anthropomorphised rabbits. So the ability to distinguish between two people of the same name, or to relate discrete items of information relating to an individual, is a key element of scholarship, albeit frequently the product of intuition and judgement.

But this identification of individuals has become much harder with the shift in historians' attentions in recent decades from the rich and famous towards populations of quite humble individuals, such as those to be found in the Westminster Historical Database, for whom reliance upon intuitive judgement is less satisfactory. Rather, it is recognised that a rule-based system must supplement intuition when linking these kinds of records. The first systematic use of rule-based record linkage was the historical demographers' family reconstitution,[2] but now a wide variety of projects have adopted record linkage strategies. The development of low-cost, high-performance computers, combined with powerful relational database management systems, has been especially conducive to this shift.

An algorithmic approach to record linkage of large data sets has two advantages over judgemental linkage of the same data. First, there is a considerable saving in time, since hand linkage is inordinately time-consuming. Secondly there is the advantage that the method used is capable of being specified. This not only increases the intellectual value of the work, but it also promotes its replicability and the possibility of comparing the results obtained with those obtained from similar data sets.[3]

There are two key stages to record linkage. The first of these involves the standardisation or coding of the contents of database fields. Without this process, low rates of record linkage are almost inevitable. In order to overcome the problems resulting from variant spellings and descriptions, the Westminster Historical Database contains several fields of standardised or coded data derived from the original historical record. Voters' surnames are also subject to a three-fold classification: the original surname string is preserved in the field *Surname*, they are standardised by the removal of vowels and repeated consonants in the field *Stdsur*, and they are given an alphanumeric code in the field *Scode*.[4] Voters' forenames are rendered similar by truncation: whilst the forename string is preserved in the field *Fname*, it is truncated to the first four characters in the field *Shtname*. As was seen in Chapter 4, the occupational classification was designed (albeit imperfectly) to bring together under a common classification items that were similar but not identical. Thus voters engaged in the coal trade may all be found in the code 'DE01', although different occupations have discrete codes at *Oclv4*. All of these codes are intended to maximise the opportunity for true linkage by rendering similar related items of data.

For example, the *Surname* strings 'ELLIOTT' and 'ELIOT' do not match but when they are standardised, either to the *Stdsur* string 'ELT' or to the *Scode* string 'E540', they can be linked. Likewise, although the *Fname* strings 'HORACE' and 'HORATIO' do not match, they nonetheless share a common *Shtname* string 'HORA'. Similarly, the *Street* strings 'SOHO SQ' and 'GREEK ST' do not match, although they were contiguous and a householder living at the northern end of Greek Street might conceivably use either; but both lay within the parish of St Anne, and so share a common *Parish* string 'A'. Finally, the *Occup* string 'COAL DEALER' will not match with the nearly-synonymous 'COAL MERCHANT', although they can be linked by their common *Oclv3* string 'DE01001'.[5]

In the second stage of record linkage, data from two or more database tables are *joined* together to form a linked data set. The important point about this exercise is that records can only be linked when they satisfy the search criteria specified in a *linkage algorithm* (generally coded in SQL as explained in Chapter 5 above). There is considerable scope for error at this stage, and it is well to remember that linkage strategies are likely to be data specific. It is thus useful to conduct experiments prior to wholesale linkage to establish the optimum techniques. Through the application of sound record linkage techniques it is possible to improve dramatically the quality of historical information retrieved, and thus to improve the quality of resulting interpretation.

Below is reported a sequence of experiments using the Westminster Historical Database to explore the characteristics of data from the tables **P1784**, **P1788**, and **R1784**, with a view to devising general linkage strategies for use with poll and rate book tables in the Database. It begins by discussing how to identify a good general-purpose linkage algorithm for linking data from poll book tables, recognising that a good algorithm is one which delivers a high yield of linked records at a high level of confidence. It then goes on to discuss the implementation of multiple pass record linkage algorithms. Using multiple pass algorithms overcomes the problem of trading off yield against confidence by delivering a higher yield than any single algorithm, but without commensurate diminution in confidence in the linked data set. Finally, it discusses some of the problems involved in linking data from rate book tables with poll book records.

It should be stressed that our discussion of record linkage is not intended to be prescriptive. It is for users of the Database to determine what linkage strategies they adopt. Rather, we seek to show some of the possible ways that the Database can be used to implement linkage of poll and rate books to form a unified data set for further analysis.

## 6.1 Confidence and returns using single algorithms

Great problems attend the identification of those who polled in successive elections, although their identification in the Database is necessary to discuss both the proportion of returning voters and their political loyalty. Winchester identified two possible sources of linkage error: the false linkage (mu error) and the failure to link those who should be linked (lambda error).[6] Both types of error are apt to occur, since the means do not exist uniquely to identify each and every Westminster voter (such as social security numbers) nor are there very strong personal identifiers (such as a combination of name and date of birth).

These problems are exacerbated by the processes of history. Westminster was not a closed community of immortals, so some voters might have participated in only one election because of migration or life-cycle events. Some might have moved into the constituency, others might have moved out of it; some might have gained eligibility to vote by becoming rate-paying householders, others might have lost eligibility by ceasing to be rate-paying householders. For each there was a time to be born and a time to die, and the pool of voters at any one time more closely resembled a pool in a flowing river than it resembled a stagnant pond. And even those voters who remained within Westminster for the duration of two elections might prove difficult to trace in both. Householders were not obliged to vote, and some may have participated in one election but abstained in others. Moreover, of those voters who participated in successive elections, some would have moved house whilst others changed their jobs. Finally, surname spelling was inconsistent whilst data drawn from printed or manuscript copies of the original poll books may contain transcription errors. Each of these will lead to a lower proportion of records being linked than might have been expected. Meanwhile, the practice of naming sons after fathers, and of those sons inheriting their fathers' estates and businesses, gives rise to the possibility of establishing false links between distinct voters.

It is difficult, therefore, to identify an obscure but interesting person such as the poet William Blake. Blake was a Westminster man, living in St James' parish in the later 1780s. Indeed, the name occurs four times in the poll books for that parish between 1784 and 1790. But only the record of the engraver of Poland Street who plumped for Fox in 1790 may confidently be ascribed to the poet, in this case because the additional data relating to occupation and place of residence is consistent with what we know of him from other sources. But Blake was by no means the most obscure citizen of Westminster in these years. Smith was by no means an uncommon surname, whilst about a fifth of the voters were called John; even the combination of names was fairly common, with 40 voters in 1788 being called John Smith.

Much attention has been devoted to the problem of linking surnames with discrepant spellings. Surname standardisation routines such as the Soundex codes incorporated into the Westminster Database, or the Guth algorithm, go some way towards eliminating these problems.[7] But other problems are more insidious. The sheer size of the constituency means that voters were less likely to be uniquely identified by name alone in Westminster than elsewhere. Moreover many householders were mobile with respect to both occupation and place of residence: Simon Place, the father of Francis Place, is just one example of the impact of life's vicissitudes on occupational and spatial mobility.[8] Compatible addresses lead on to further problems: if a voter's house lay at the corner of two streets, then he might use one address in the first election and subsequently use the other. Meanwhile, some properties ran from a main thoroughfare to a back street, giving further scope for confusion of addresses.[9] Finally, the problem is compounded by incomplete data. Whilst use of the manuscript poll books for Westminster has considerable advantages, it suffers from the key disadvantage that not all of them have survived. This can be seen from a comparison of the voting figures shown in Table 3.4 with those shown in Tables 3.5 to 3.16. It was thus possible for a voting record to be list unique and linked at the level of name and parish between two poll book tables, not because the voter was the only one of that name to have polled in the parish but simply because of the contingency of data survival. This problem is clearly most acute for those elections where loss of data has been greatest, and may even preclude linkage across parishes where data for one parish have not survived.

The ability of relational database management systems to retrieve information from one or more tables with a single command makes them particularly suitable for the linkage of relatively highly structured data such as that in the Westminster Historical Database.

Using a relational database management system to hold information in two-way tables means that there are many methods by which information from different tables may be linked. Each method of linkage may be implemented by using a different algorithm. When linking records from two poll book tables in the Westminster Historical Database there are 45 different algorithms which might be implemented. Each of these algorithms carries a different level of confidence, and each returns a different number of linked records. Selecting the optimum single algorithm to link records from two tables may involve a trade-off between returns and confidence.

Records are linked by attributes that define an entity. If the entity is a voter, he might be defined by the attributes of **Name**, **Place** and **Occupation**. Each algorithm may be thought of as being built up from component parts relating to **Name** (N), **Place of residence** (P), and **Occupation** (O). There are three keys relating to **Name**, two relating to **Place** and four relating to **Occupation**. These components may be implemented in combination to produce a variety of linkage keys. Assuming that records must match on at least Name (using the shortened form of the forename throughout), this gives a total of 45 available record linkage algorithms. The component keys of linkage algorithms are shown below in Table 6.1.

**Table 6.1 Definition of poll book record linkage keys**

| Code | Definition |
|------|-----------|
| N1 | surname + shortened forename |
| N2 | standardised surname + shortened forename |
| N3 | Russell Soundex code of surname string + shortened forename |
| P1 | parish + street |
| P2 | parish |
| O1 | economic sector (Booth/Armstrong classification) |
| O2 | economic sub-sector (Booth/Armstrong classification) |
| O3 | trade cluster |
| O4 | stated occupation |

The possible combination of keys in record linkage algorithms are ranked later in this chapter in Table 6.2. The 45 available algorithms correspond to the four original groups as follows:

| N | | = 3 |
|---|---|---|
| N + P | 3 x 2 | = 6 |
| N + O | 3 x 4 | = 12 |
| N + P + O | 3 x 2 x 4 | = 24 |

The idea of list uniqueness is central to much of the literature on record linkage, and it is useful to give a brief overview of the concept and its implications before continuing to apply the concept in the record linkage exercise which follows. The problem stems from the size of the Westminster electorate, in consequence of which not all voters were distinguishable by means of their names, addresses and occupations; and still fewer could be distinguished when using fewer identifying criteria (such as surname and forename). To return to our earlier example, if we sought information on the voting behaviour of the poet and artist William Blake, who is known to have lived in St James's parish in the later eighteenth century, a search of the tables **P1774**, **P1784**, **P1788** and **P1790** using the query

```
WHERE Surname = 'BLAKE'
AND Shtname = 'WILL'
AND Parish = 'D'
```

will yield the following records:

| Table | Fname | Surname | Street | Occup | Vote | Rate |
|---|---|---|---|---|---|---|
| P1774 | William | Blake | Berwick St | Gent | 11000 | |
| | William | Blake | Marshall St | Poulterer | 11000 | |
| P1784 | William | Blake | Berwick St | Gent | 001 | |
| | William | Blake | Windmill St | Carpenter | 110 | |
| R1784 | William | Blake | Windmill St | | | 16 |
| | William | Blake | Berwick St | | | 40 |
| P1790 | William | Blake | Poland St | Engraver | 100 | |
| | William | Blake | Berwick St | Gent | 100 | |

The results suggest that there were probably four householders in St James's parish during this period of just sixteen years who had the surname and forename combination 'William Blake'. There was the gentleman of Berwick Street, rated at £40; there was the poulterer of Marshall Street; there was the carpenter of Windmill Street, rated at £16; and there was William Blake of Poland Street, engraver, who was surely the poet. None of these householders was list unique at the level of *Surname*, *Fname* and *Parish*; indeed, their homes were so clustered in that part of Soho which lay within St James's parish that they might have met. However, when additional distinguishing criteria are added (in this case, *Street* and *Occup*) it becomes possible to distinguish between the eponymous but distinct voters.

Because of the principle of the *identity of indistinguishables* it is impossible to distinguish between two individuals in the table **P1784** with common character strings in the fields *Surname*, *Shtname*, *Parish*, *Street*, and *Oclv4*.[10] It is thus necessary to eliminate these multiple entries prior to linkage by creating a subset of each table offered for linkage containing only those records which are list unique on the selected linkage criteria. This must be done for each linkage algorithm implemented, eliminating different records (and thus creating a different subset of list unique cases) with the implementation of each algorithm-specific list unique clause.

The algorithm which *a priori* was held to be the strongest was that which had fewest records eliminated as being non list unique, whilst the one which *a priori* was held to be the weakest was the one which had the greatest number of records eliminated as being non list unique. This was held to be the product of neither accident nor inexplicable coincidence, but a function of the relationship between the probability of a record being list unique and our confidence in linkages made using the algorithm which had established the list uniqueness of that record. We can thus derive an index of relative confidence from the data itself.

Having derived a method of ranking the 45 available algorithms by our confidence in them, according to the proportion of records eliminated by the list unique clause for each from the table **P1784**, we may go on to consider the yield of each linkage algorithm in turn. The yield is simply the number of records linked by each algorithm from the list unique subset for that algorithm of tables **P1784** and **P1788**. The number of linked cases for an algorithm is found out first by making list unique versions of each table for that algorithm as described above.

In the first instance, then, we need to find out how much confidence we have in each linkage algorithm. This can be done by implementing each (algorithm-specific) list unique clause for table **P1784**, and then ranking the 45 algorithms in order of their strength.[11] The following SQL command will create a subset of the data held in **P1784** which are list unique in the fields *Surname*, *Shtname, Parish, Street* and *Oclv4*.

```
CREATE TABLE P1784TEMP1
AS SELECT Surname, Shtname, Parish, Street,
Oclv4
FROM P1784
GROUP BY Surname, Shtname, Parish, Street,
Oclv4
HAVING COUNT(*)=1;
```

This subset of the data held in **P1784** is a table called **P1784TEMP1**. It contains 11,387 records, having eliminated just 40 records from **P1784** as being non list unique. In other words, over 99.6 per cent of the 11,427 poll book cases in **P1784** had survived the implementation of the list unique clause. By contrast, the list unique clause for Algorithm 45 eliminated 6,182 records, or 54.1 per cent of the records in **P1784**. The table **P1784TEMP45** was used to link only those list unique records with matching character strings in the fields of *Scode* and *Shtname*.

The resulting tables **P1784TEMP1** and **P1788TEMP1,** which are list unique subsets of tables **P1784** and **P1788**, can now be linked using Algorithm 1. This is done by implementing the following query:

```
SELECT COUNT(*) FROM P1784TEMP1, P1788TEMP1
WHERE P1784TEMP1.Surname =
P1788TEMP1.Surname
AND P1784TEMP1.Shtname = P1788TEMP1.Shtname
AND P1784TEMP1.Parish = P1788TEMP1.Parish
AND P1784TEMP1.Street = P1788TEMP1.Street
AND P1784TEMP1.Oclv4 = P1788TEMP1.Oclv4;
```

This would give us the result that just 1,674 cases were common to both tables. Implementing linkage queries for each of the 45 available algorithms shows that the number of linked records yielded by a single algorithm lay in a range between 1,674 and 2,868. Perhaps unsurprisingly, it was the algorithm with the highest confidence level that had the lowest yield. But there was no direct relationship between confidence and yield: indeed, the second-lowest yield came from the algorithm in which we had least confidence. The highest yield, of 34.9 per cent, came from Algorithm 39, linking records having common character strings in the fields *Stdsur*, *Shtname* and *Parish*.

Another noteworthy feature of the table showing confidence and yield for each algorithm is that over half of the algorithms operated at a confidence level of over 98 per cent, and that less than one tenth operated at a confidence level lower than 75 per cent. This clustering of confidence meant that for many algorithms the key variable was yield.

To find the optimum single algorithm it is necessary to regress the percentage of linked records for each algorithm (x axis) on the confidence in the links made thereby (y axis). This measure of confidence was the proportion of records from **P1784** which had survived the implementation of the list unique clause for that algorithm. The regression residuals are distributed binomially when the algorithms are implemented in rank order, as shown in Table 6.2. The optimum single algorithm, Algorithm 39, has the highest positive residual (albeit at a relatively low level of confidence) and is highlighted in Table 6.2. However, the regression line was virtually flat, so that the optimum trade-off between confidence and yield was largely a function of yield. It will be noted that in Table 6.2, which ranks the algorithms by their robustness, it is not until Algorithm 25 is reached that we are using an algorithm which does not incorporate parish of residence as a linkage key.

**Table 6.2 Ranking and returns to the 45 available poll book linkage algorithms**

| No. | Definition | No. of List Unique Records in 1784 | Records List Unique (%) * | Records Linked by Single Algorithm | Standard Linkage Rate (%)** | Residual |
|---|---|---|---|---|---|---|
| 1 | N1+P1+O4 | 11,387 | 99.6 | 1,674 | 20.4 | -8.68 |
| 2 | N1+P1+O3 | 11,385 | 99.6 | 1,823 | 22.2 | -6.87 |
| 3 | N2+P1+O4 | 11,383 | 99.6 | 1,968 | 23.9 | -5.10 |
| 4 | N1+P1+O2 | 11,383 | 99.6 | 1,888 | 23.0 | -6.08 |
| 5 | N2+P1+O3 | 11,379 | 99.6 | 2,151 | 26.1 | -2.88 |
| 6 | N2+P1+O2 | 11,375 | 99.5 | 2,230 | 27.1 | -1.92 |
| 7 | N3+P1+O4 | 11,373 | 99.5 | 2,046 | 24.9 | -4.15 |
| 8 | N1+P1+O1 | 11,367 | 99.5 | 2,016 | 24.5 | -4.52 |
| 9 | N3+P1+O3 | 11,365 | 99.5 | 2,234 | 27.2 | -1.87 |
| 10 | N3+P1+O2 | 11,361 | 99.4 | 2,315 | 28.1 | -0.88 |
| 11 | N2+P1+O1 | 11,359 | 99.4 | 2,374 | 28.9 | -0.16 |
| 12 | N3+P1+O1 | 11,331 | 99.2 | 2,461 | 29.9 | 0.90 |
| 13 | N1+P1 | 11,324 | 99.1 | 2,289 | 27.8 | -1.19 |
| 14 | N1+P2+O4 | 11,312 | 99.0 | 2,017 | 24.5 | -4.50 |
| 15 | N2+P1 | 11,312 | 99.0 | 2,691 | 32.7 | 3.70 |
| 16 | N1+P2+O3 | 11,302 | 98.9 | 2,201 | 26.8 | -2.26 |
| 17 | N2+P2+O4 | 11,296 | 98.9 | 2,347 | 28.5 | -0.48 |
| 18 | N2+P2+O3 | 11,284 | 98.7 | 2,570 | 31.2 | 2.23 |
| 19 | N3+P1 | 11,250 | 98.5 | 2,787 | 33.9 | 4.88 |
| 20 | N3+P2+O4 | 11,249 | 98.4 | 2,438 | 29.6 | 0.63 |
| 21 | N1+P2+O2 | 11,227 | 98.2 | 2,263 | 27.5 | -1.49 |
| 22 | N3+P2+O3 | 11,226 | 98.2 | 2,664 | 32.4 | 3.39 |
| 23 | N2+P2+O2 | 11,201 | 98.0 | 2,649 | 32.2 | 3.21 |
| 24 | N3+P2+O2 | 11,106 | 97.2 | 2,733 | 33.2 | 4.25 |
| 25 | N1+O4 | 11,098 | 97.1 | 2,117 | 25.7 | -3.24 |
| 26 | N1+O3 | 11,036 | 96.6 | 2,302 | 28.0 | -0.98 |
| 27 | N2+O4 | 11,017 | 96.4 | 2,447 | 29.7 | 0.79 |
| 28 | N1+P2+O1 | 10,954 | 95.9 | 2,374 | 28.9 | -0.09 |
| 29 | N2+O3 | 10,937 | 95.7 | 2,664 | 32.4 | 3.44 |
| 30 | N2+P2+O1 | 10,828 | 94.8 | 2,749 | 33.4 | 4.49 |
| 31 | N3+O4 | 10,825 | 94.7 | 2,532 | 30.8 | 1.85 |
| 32 | N1+O2 | 10,804 | 94.5 | 2,356 | 28.6 | -0.28 |
| 33 | N3+O3 | 10,698 | 93.6 | 2,742 | 33.3 | 4.43 |

| No. | Definition | No. of List Unique Records in 1784 | Records List Unique (%) * | Records Linked by Single Algorithm | Standard Linkage Rate (%)** | Residual |
|-----|-----------|-----------|-----------|-----------|-----------|-----------|
| 34 | N2+O2 | 10,650 | 93.2 | 2,733 | 33.2 | 4.33 |
| 35 | N3+P2+O1 | 10,512 | 92.0 | 2,810 | 34.2 | 5.29 |
| 36 | N3+O2 | 10,243 | 89.6 | 2,751 | 33.4 | 4.62 |
| 37 | N1+P2 | 10,111 | 88.5 | 2,508 | 30.5 | 1.69 |
| 38 | N1+O1 | 9,899 | 86.6 | 2,305 | 28.0 | -0.74 |
| **39** | **N2+P2** | **9,721** | **85.1** | **2,868** | **34.9** | **6.14** |
| 40 | N2+O1 | 9,453 | 82.7 | 2,620 | 31.9 | 3.18 |
| 41 | N3+P2 | 8,756 | 76.6 | 2,704 | 32.9 | 4.33 |
| 42 | N3+O1 | 8,384 | 73.4 | 2,461 | 29.9 | 1.44 |
| 43 | N1 | 8,098 | 70.9 | 2,084 | 25.3 | -3.09 |
| 44 | N2 | 7,085 | 62.0 | 2,227 | 27.1 | -1.17 |
| 45 | N3 | 5,245 | 45.9 | 1,753 | 21.3 | -6.59 |

\* Total population in 1784 = 11,427
\*\* % of 1788 population = 8,226

## Figure 6.1 Relative confidence in individual algorithms

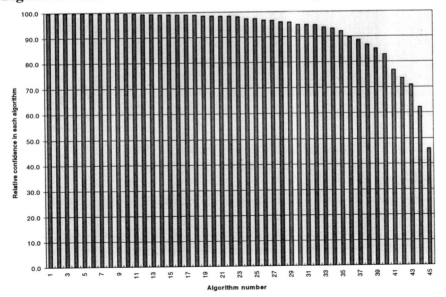

**Figure 6.2 Yield of individual algorithms**

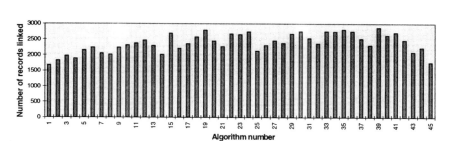

**Figure 6.3 Regression residuals of confidence on yield of individual algorithms**

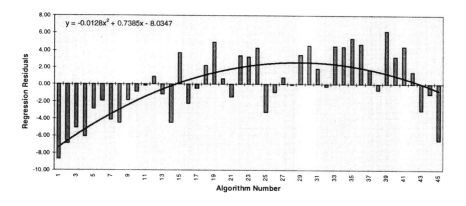

We may seek an explanation for the strength and stability of parish and street as strong and stable identifiers of individuals in two elements of the historical process of electioneering. Firstly, parishes were used as units of political organisation throughout the period: whilst candidates maintained central committees in Covent Garden during elections much of the work of canvassing electors and bringing them to poll was delegated to parish-based committees, and between elections voter loyalty was maintained through parochial political clubs.[12] Secondly, poll books were used for canvassing, enabling the agents to identify potential supporters.[13] Printed poll books ordered by street within each parish, such as that from the Westminster election of 1780, were especially conducive to this. It is in part these emphases upon the names and addresses of the voters that helps to explain the relative strength of names and addresses as identifiers of individual voters.

No matter how discriminating the algorithm implemented, the researcher can never claim with complete confidence that all the records in a unified data set represent true linkage. The world inhabited by historians is simply too messy and roughly-hewn for that. After all, the voter may have died and been replaced by another of the same name, address, and occupation. It seems unlikely that any voter from 1749 could have survived to poll in the election of 1818, so links established between these two poll books may be held to be false. Even using Algorithm 1 to link records with common character strings in the fields *Surname*, *Shtname*, *Parish*, *Street*, and *Oclv4* between the tables **P1749** and **P1818**, links were nevertheless made for three voters. Meanwhile, the least discriminating algorithm, linking records with matching character strings on the fields *Scode* and *Shtname*, established links between 682 pairs of voters in 1789 and 1818, or more than one in eight of those at risk.

## 6.2 Implementing multiple pass record linkage algorithms[14]

Using multiple pass algorithms overcomes the difficulty of the trade-off between yield and confidence encountered using single algorithms. It requires exhaustive querying of the Database, but this is not unduly onerous once the temporary tables containing common records have been set up. A total of 45 algorithms are available to link data from Tables **P1784** and **P1788**, assuming that the minimum requirement for linkage is matching on both elements of personal names, that *Shtname* is used throughout for forename strings, and that information in the *Vote* field is not used for linkage purposes. Multiple pass algorithms are implemented by using the command UNION to create complex queries which link data by using successively weaker linkage criteria. A worked example of the process is given below in section 6.3; meanwhile, the key point to note is that implementing multiple pass algorithms dramatically increases the number of linked records yielded without greatly reducing overall confidence in the linked data set.

**Table 6.3 Cumulative increase in records linked through application of multiple pass procedure**

| No. | Definition | Additional No. of Records Linked | Cumulative Total | Standard Linkage Rate (%)* |
|---|---|---|---|---|
| 1 | N1+P1+O4 | 1,674 | 1,674 | 20.4 |
| 2 | N1+P1+O3 | 151 | 1,825 | 22.2 |
| 3 | N2+P1+O4 | 296 | 2,121 | 25.8 |
| 4 | N1+P1+O2 | 66 | 2,187 | 26.6 |
| 5 | N2+P1+O3 | 34 | 2,221 | 27.0 |
| 6 | N2+P1+O2 | 14 | 2,235 | 27.2 |
| 7 | N3+P1+O4 | 88 | 2,323 | 28.2 |
| 8 | N1+P1+O1 | 134 | 2,457 | 29.9 |
| 9 | N3+P1+O3 | 8 | 2,465 | 30.0 |
| 10 | N3+P1+O2 | 2 | 2,467 | 30.0 |
| 11 | N2+P1+O1 | 16 | 2,483 | 30.2 |
| 12 | N3+P1+O1 | 9 | 2,492 | 30.3 |
| 13 | N1+P1 | 288 | 2,780 | 33.8 |
| 14 | N1+P2+O4 | 363 | 3,143 | 38.2 |
| 15 | N2+P1 | 47 | 3,190 | 38.8 |
| 16 | N1+P2+O3 | 42 | 3,232 | 39.3 |
| 17 | N2+P2+O4 | 46 | 3,278 | 39.8 |
| 18 | N2+P2+O3 | 6 | 3,284 | 39.9 |
| 19 | N3+P1 | 20 | 3,304 | 40.2 |
| 20 | N3+P2+O4 | 34 | 3,338 | 40.6 |
| 21 | N1+P2+O2 | 27 | 3,365 | 40.9 |
| 22 | N3+P2+O3 | 4 | 3,369 | 41.0 |
| 23 | N2+P2+O2 | 12 | 3,381 | 41.1 |
| 24 | N3+P2+O2 | 12 | 3,393 | 41.2 |
| 25 | N1+O4 | 177 | 3,570 | 43.4 |
| 26 | N1+O3 | 29 | 3,599 | 43.8 |
| 27 | N2+O4 | 35 | 3,634 | 44.2 |
| 28 | N1+P2+O1 | 86 | 3,720 | 45.2 |
| 29 | N2+O3 | 3 | 3,723 | 45.3 |
| 30 | N2+P2+O1 | 27 | 3,750 | 45.6 |
| 31 | N3+O4 | 54 | 3,804 | 46.2 |
| 32 | N1+O2 | 57 | 3,861 | 46.9 |

| No. | Definition | Additional No. of Records Linked | Cumulative Total | Standard Linkage Rate (%)* |
|-----|------------|----------------------------------|------------------|----------------------------|
| 33 | N3+O3 | 11 | 3,872 | 47.1 |
| 34 | N2+O2 | 24 | 3,896 | 47.4 |
| 35 | N3+P2+O1 | 69 | 3,965 | 48.2 |
| 36 | N3+O2 | 39 | 4,004 | 48.7 |
| 37 | N1+P2 | 217 | 4,221 | 51.3 |
| 38 | N1+O1 | 153 | 4,374 | 53.2 |
| 39 | N2+P2 | 86 | 4,460 | 54.2 |
| 40 | N2+O1 | 46 | 4,506 | 54.8 |
| 41 | N3+P2 | 117 | 4,623 | 56.2 |
| 42 | N3+O1 | 87 | 4,710 | 57.3 |
| 43 | N1 | 177 | 4,887 | 59.4 |
| 44 | N2 | 93 | 4,980 | 60.5 |
| 45 | N3 | 125 | 5,105 | 62.1 |

* % of 1788 population = 8,226

**Figure 6.4 Total number of records linked with progression of multiple pass procedure**

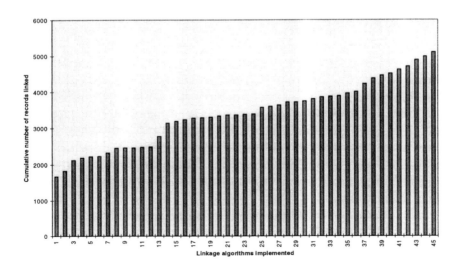

**Figure 6.5 Change in relative confidence with progression of multiple pass procedure**

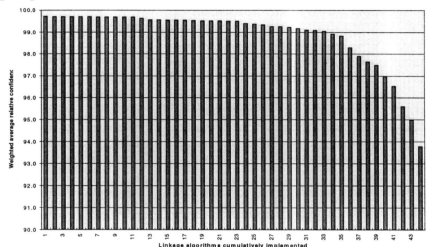

Looking at Figure 6.4, showing the total number of records linked with the progression of the multiple pass procedure, it will be seen that while the trend approximates to a straight line, closer inspection reveals a series of steps and terraces. Thus implementation of Algorithms 9 through 12 added just 35 records, whilst implementation of Algorithms 13 and 14 added 651. Terraces are caused by the slackening of a linkage key, whilst steps are caused by the removal of a linkage key. If the algorithms were implemented individually, then removal of a linkage key would be reflected in a marked diminution in confidence in the linked data set. But when the algorithms are implemented iteratively, confidence in the linked data set as a whole does not fall below 99 per cent until the thirty-fifth iteration. Indeed, it is around the thirty-fifth iteration that weighted average confidence in the linked data set drops below 99 per cent, and Algorithm 36 is the first which, implemented individually, delivers records at a confidence level of less than 90 per cent.

Nevertheless, there would still be some records which remained unlinked although the case for linkage might appear strong: Algorithm 37, for example, will yield the records of voters who have changed both their occupation and their place of residence within a parish.[15] The forty-fifth iteration yielded 5,105 linked records, or approximately three-fifths of the records in **P1788**. It thus yielded about three times as many linked records as Algorithm 1 alone. Moreover, the forty-fifth iteration delivered this abundance of linked records at an average weighted confidence of 94 per cent. Whilst we do not prescribe running all iterations, we recommend experimenting with multiple pass procedures.

## 6.3 An application of record linkage using the Westminster Historical Database

Record linkage enables us to probe beneath the surface of the historical record to ask important historical questions. To take one example: the change in the political representation of Westminster, from returning one Whig and one Administration candidate in the general election of 1784 to returning a second Whig candidate in the by-election of 1788, was attributable to a number of factors. Defeated candidates at by-elections today commonly explain their failure in terms of differential turnout: 'our people abstained as a protest'. But this is unlikely to have been important in 1788, when with 11,961 electors recorded as having polled over fifteen days the constituency came close to polling out. More important were life-cycle processes such as the replacement of some voters from the cohort of 1784 with new and inexperienced voters in the later contest. But in addition the overall change was the product of a net change in behaviour by those who participated in both elections. So to begin to explain the change in Westminster's political representation in the period 1784 to 1788 we would wish to know how many of the voters in 1788 were newcomers, and how many of them had participated in the election of 1784.

The number of cases common to both tables using the linkage criteria of having common character strings in the fields *Surname*, *Shtname*, *Parish*, *Street* and *Oclv4* gives a lower bound of around a fifth of the voters in 1788 who had prior experience, and thus around four-fifths who were newcomers to the hustings. This is a simple query to show the possibilities of record linkage: in reality, the proportion of experienced electors at the hustings would have been substantially greater. Nonetheless, much of the change in political representation of the constituency in the 1780s may thus be attributed to the turnover of electoral cohorts. But some was attributable to change in the behaviour of individuals who partici-pated in both elections. To retrieve this behaviour it is useful to create a further temporary table containing information relating to those who participated in both elections, having common character strings in the fields *Surname*, *Shtname*, *Parish*, *Street*, and *Oclv4* in tables **P1784** and **P1788**:

```
CREATE TABLE P84_88TEMP1
AS SELECT P1784TEMP1.Surname,
P1784TEMP1.Shtname,
P1784TEMP1.Parish, P1784TEMP1.Street,
P1784TEMP1.Oclv4
FROM P1784TEMP1, P1788TEMP1
WHERE P1784TEMP1.Surname =
P1788TEMP1.Surname
AND P1784TEMP1.Shtname = P1788TEMP1.Shtname
AND P1784TEMP1.Parish = P1788TEMP1.Parish
AND P1784TEMP1.Street = P1788TEMP1.Street
AND P1784TEMP1.Oclv4 = P1788TEMP1.Oclv4;
```

Once this temporary table has been created, cases contained in it can be linked with those in the tables **P1784** and **P1788**, which contain   information concerning voting behaviour. This rather complicated procedure is necessary because *Vote* data cannot be included when making the list unique subsets of the original tables.

```
CREATE TABLE P84_88VOTE1
AS SELECT P1784.Vote, P1788.Vote
FROM P84_88TEMP1, P1784, P1788
WHERE P84_88TEMP1.Surname = P1784.Surname
AND P84_88TEMP1.Shtname = P1784.Shtname
AND P84_88TEMP1.Parish = P1784.Parish
AND P84_88TEMP1.Street = P1784.Street
AND P84_88TEMP1.Oclv4 = P1784.Oclv4
AND P84_88TEMP1.Surname = P1788.Surname
AND P84_88TEMP1.Shtname = P1788.Shtname
AND P84_88TEMP1.Parish = P1788.Parish
AND P84_88TEMP1.Street = P1788.Street
AND P84_88TEMP1.Oclv4 = P1788.Oclv4;
```

Table 6.4 shows the transition matrix of voting behaviour of those who participated in the elections of 1784 and 1788 and who were linked by common character strings in the fields *Surname*, *Shtname, Parish, Street* and *Oclv4*.

**Table 6.4 Voting behaviour in 1784 and 1788, linked by Algorithm 1**

|  | Hood & Wray | Hood & Fox | Hood | Wray & Fox | Wray | Fox | Total |
|---|---|---|---|---|---|---|---|
| **Hood** | 694 | 48 | 14 | 8 | 17 | 129 | **910** |
| **Townshend** | 149 | 96 | 6 | 4 | 7 | 502 | **764** |
| **Total** | **843** | **144** | **20** | **12** | **24** | **631** | **1,674** |

**Table 6.5 Voting in 1788 by electoral experience, linked by Algorithm 1**

|  | Hood | | Townshend | |
|---|---|---|---|---|
| Experienced | 910 | 23 % | 764 | 18 % |
| Newcomers | 3,037 | 77 % | 3,515 | 82 % |
| **Total** | **3,947** | | **4,279** | |

Implementing a relatively straightforward series of commands and queries has thus enabled us to extract information about those who polled in both 1784 and 1788. Close examination of Table 6.4 shows that, although only a fifth of the voters in 1788 have been traced as having voted in 1784, nonetheless they were remarkable for their political consistency. Nearly three quarters of the linked voters polled either for Hood and Wray in 1784, followed by Hood in 1788, or they polled for Fox in 1784 followed by Townshend in 1788.

Moreover floating voting in one direction was virtually cancelled out by those who floated in the opposite direction, and the net impact of floating voting was slight. Whilst 129 of those who had plumped for Fox in 1784 polled for Hood in 1788, there were 149 who polled for Townshend in that year who had polled for Hood and Wray four years earlier. The overwhelming impression given by Table 6.4 is of political consistency over time, lending support to an argument explaining political change largely in terms of the recruitment of new voters.

However, the linked data set tabulated in Table 6.4 is unrepresentative of the voters in **P1788**. Whereas in fact 52 per cent of the voters in **P1788** polled for Townshend, only 46 per cent of the linked voters analysed in Table 6.4 did so. Whether this was because Townshend's Whig camp was better at recruiting new voters, or whether it was because their voters were more mobile (either occupationally or spatially, since either would preclude linkage by Algorithm 1) than Hood's men, remains to be seen.

This explanation of political change in terms of the recruitment of new voters can be seen most clearly if the voters in 1788 are classified by whether they were experienced or were newcomers, as shown in Table 6.5.

Implementing Algorithm 39, the optimum single linkage algorithm, still lends broad support to an explanation of change in the political representation of Westminster in terms of recruitment of new voters, since members of the cohort of 1784 who returned to poll were broadly consistent and the net impact of floating voting was slight (see Table 6.6). However, it also suggests that recruitment of new voters was less important than had been suggested by implementing Algorithm 1, and that rather greater emphasis should be placed upon the Whigs' conversion of returning voters (see Table 6.7). It is shown, then, that historical explanation may vary according to the computational methods adopted.

**Table 6.6 Voting behaviour in 1784 and 1788, linked by Algorithm 39**

|            | Hood & Wray | Hood & Fox | Hood | Wray & Fox | Wray | Fox   | Total     |
|------------|-------------|------------|------|------------|------|-------|-----------|
| **Hood**      | 1,111       | 85         | 22   | 13         | 41   | 231   | **1,503** |
| **Townshend** | 293         | 132        | 9    | 8          | 14   | 909   | **1,365** |
| **Total**     | **1,404**   | **217**    | **31** | **21**   | **55** | **1,140** | **2,868** |

**Table 6.7 Voting in 1788 by electoral experience, linked by Algorithm 39**

|             | **Hood** |      | **Townshend** |      |
|-------------|----------|------|---------------|------|
| Experienced | 1,503    | 38 % | 1,365         | 32 % |
| Newcomers   | 2,444    | 62 % | 2,914         | 68 % |
| **Total**   | **3,947**|      | **4,279**     |      |

We may carry this argument further through the use of a multiple pass algorithm in preference to the single algorithm applied thus far. A more complex multiple pass algorithm might begin by linking those cases with matching strings in the fields *Surname*, *Shtname*, *Parish*, *Street* and *Oclv4*. It would then link cases using multiple passes, each one implementing a progressively less discriminating algorithm, until the 45th iteration is reached which links cases matching on character strings in the fields *Scode* and *Shtname* which have not previously been linked. The example below uses Algorithms 44 and 45 for no better reason than to save space, and it illustrates the use of the command UNION:

```
CREATE TABLE P84_88VOTE44_45 (VOTE84,
VOTE88, PARISH84, LINENO84, PARISH88,
LINENO88)
AS SELECT P1784.VOTE, P1788.VOTE,
P1784.PARISH, P1784.LINENO, P1788.PARISH,
P1788.LINENO
FROM P84_88TEMP44, P1784, P1788
WHERE P84_88TEMP44.STDSUR=P1784.STDSUR
AND P84_88TEMP44.SHTNAME=P1784.SHTNAME
AND P84_88TEMP44.STDSUR=P1788.STDSUR
AND P84_88TEMP44.SHTNAME=P1788.SHTNAME
UNION
SELECT P1784.VOTE, P1788.VOTE, P1784.PARISH,
P1784.LINENO, P1788.PARISH, P1788.LINENO
FROM P84_88TEMP45, P1784, P1788
WHERE P84_88TEMP45.SCODE=P1784.SCODE
AND P84_88TEMP45.SHTNAME=P1784.SHTNAME
AND P84_88TEMP45.SCODE=P1788.SCODE
AND P84_88TEMP45.SHTNAME=P1788.SHTNAME;
```

The results of implementing a full 45 iterations of the multiple pass procedure are presented in Tables 6.8 and 6.9. Analysis of Table 6.8 suggests that both the Whigs and the Administration retained more voters than had been suggested by the implementation of Algorithm 1 alone. Conversely, neither was so good at recruiting new electors as the results from Algorithm 1 suggested. Moreover, of those who participated in both elections, a smaller proportion were consistent than had at first sight appeared. As shown by Table

6.3, 82 per cent of those who had polled for Hood and Wray in 1784 polled for Hood in 1788, whilst 80 per cent of those who plumped for Fox in 1784 polled for Townshend four years later. But Table 6.8 suggests that the incidence of consistency was lower: 72 per cent of those who polled for Hood and Wray in 1784 voted for Hood in 1788, whilst 74 per cent of those who plumped for Fox in 1784 polled for Townshend four years later.

**Table 6.8 Voting behaviour in 1784 and 1788, linked by Algorithms 1-45**

|           | Hood<br>& Wray | Hood<br>& Fox | Hood | Wray<br>& Fox | Wray | Fox   | Total |
|-----------|---------------|--------------|------|--------------|------|-------|-------|
| Hood      | 1,754         | 146          | 32   | 20           | 63   | 538   | **2,553** |
| Townshend | 673           | 235          | 23   | 14           | 49   | 1,558 | **2,552** |
| **Total** | **2,427**     | **381**      | **55** | **34**     | **112** | **2,096** | **5,105** |

**Table 6.9 Voting in 1788 by electoral experience, linked by Algorithms 1-45**

|             | Hood      |      | Townshend |      |
|-------------|-----------|------|-----------|------|
| Experienced | 2,553     | 65 % | 2,552     | 60 % |
| Newcomers   | 1,394     | 35 % | 1,727     | 40 % |
| **Total**   | **3,947** |      | **4,279** |      |

Table 6.8 suggests that floating voting was more common than had been suggested by Table 6.4, and that the net beneficiary of this was Townshend. To be sure, some of those who polled for Hood and Fox in 1784 may have been Foxite Whigs who were reluctant to waste their second vote, and so might be expected to drift towards the Whig camp when forced to make a choice. But substantially more former supporters of Hood and Wray shifted towards Townshend in 1788 than former Fox plumpers shifted towards Hood.

Townshend's victory over Hood in the by-election of 1788 was not attributable to any single factor. The Whig camp was better at recruiting new voters than their Administration rivals; the Whigs were also better able to retain the allegiance of their core supporters, the Foxite plumpers of 1784, than the Administration camp was able to retain the allegiance of the larger cohort of Hood-Wray straight voters; finally the Whigs were able to persuade more of their former opponents to switch to their side than the Administration camp was able to persuade former Whigs to float.

This example has shown the importance of record linkage in adding value to the data by yielding additional information. It has also shown how the results, and thus the sort of explanation of historical processes which might be advanced by historians, are dependent upon the methods adopted. However, the key point is illustrated by Figures 6.4 and 6.5: that implementation of multiple pass record linkage algorithms delivers a dramatic increase in the number of records linked, at the cost of only a small diminution in confidence in the resulting data set as a whole.

## 6.4 Linkage of poll book and rate book records

Linkage of poll and rate book data presents a different set of problems to linkage of poll book records. In some respects the linkage strategies are simpler: electors were entitled to vote by virtue of their having been assessed for the Poor Rate, and so we might expect a high degree of correspondence between the two sources. In particular, linkage is necessarily intra-parochial: it is true that particularly well-off people might have had property in more than one parish. For example, Henry Townley Ward was a prominent Foxite Whig who lived in Soho Square in St Anne's parish in the later 1780s. He was also a lawyer by profession, with an office in Covent Garden. But linking individuals across parish boundaries becomes hopelessly complicated for those possessed of less outlandish names, and so in practice linkage of poll and rate book data must take place within the parish. Moreover, rate books lack occupational data. So the available keys for record linkage using poll and rate books are **Name** and **Place**.

When linking poll books, the key **Name** can be operated at three levels. However with rate books there are six potential levels at which the key **Name** might be operated. In addition to the familiar keys N1, N2 and N3, indicating a variety of surname string (*Surname*, *Stdsur* or *Scode*) in combination with *Shtname*, rate book data are frequently found without forenames. These may be called N4 (*Surname* where *Shtname* is null), N5 (*Stdsur* where

*Shtname* is null), and N6 (*Scode* where *Shtname* is null). These rate book entries were in the form 'Smith' or 'Mr Smith' at a given address, and whilst a non-matching string in the forename field would clearly preclude linkage, the grounds for precluding linkage where one field is null are less certain. Nor is this a trivial problem: about 18 per cent of the records in the table **R1784**, and 16 per cent in the table **R1818**, have null values in the forename field.

The other distinction between poll books and rate books in record linkage terms was that whilst electors only voted once (at any rate in theory), it was quite possible for a householder to be rated on more than one property within a parish, or even within a street. Excluding the attempt to link all available rate book data relating to an elector, there are three ways of linking data which match at the levels of **Name** and **Place**. In the first case, the rate book entry may be list unique; indeed, by far the majority of rate book entries fall into this category. Secondly, if the rate book entry is non list unique, the highest value at a given address may be selected. Thirdly, if the highest value at a given address is not list unique, then one example of the highest value entry may be linked.

There are thus 54 possible ways of linking a list unique poll book record to its counterpart in the rate books:

**N**          6 x 3        = 18
**N + P**      6 x 3 x 2    = 36

Nevertheless, there remain problems for the linkage of poll and rate books depending upon the treatment of place of residence. These problems may be illustrated by the case of Benjamin Allen, a butcher of Newport Market in St Anne's parish who polled in 1784. Allen doubtless had a stall in Newport Market, and gave this address when he polled. But he also had a house in nearby Newport Street, and the house unsurprisingly had a higher rateable value than the stall.

| Table | Forename | Surname | Street | Occupation | Vote | Rate |
|-------|----------|---------|--------|------------|------|------|
| P1784 | Benjamin | Allen | Newport Mkt | Butcher | 110 | |
| R1784 | Benjamin | Allen | Newport Mkt | | | 12 |
| R1784 | Benjamin | Allen | Newport St | | | 32 |

Ultimately, the user of the Database must determine what record linkage strategies to adopt. We have deliberately sought not to be prescriptive, but rather to advocate a 'horses for courses' approach. Record linkage experiments will quickly suggest what is an appropriate linkage strategy for each case, and it may well be that the majority of cases are most easily dealt with by some variety of 'Name and Place' linkage. However, our experience leads us to urge more advanced users to adopt multiple pass algorithms for both poll-poll and poll-rate linkage as these offer dramatically improved results at but small marginal cost.

*Notes*

1       For useful overviews of the importance of record linkage, and of linkage strategies, see C. Harvey and J. Press, *Databases in historical research: theory, methods and applications* (Basingstoke, 1996) pp. 234-52, and I. Winchester, 'What every historian needs to know about record linkage in the microcomputer era', *Historical Methods*, 25 (1992), pp. 149-65.

2       See E.A. Wrigley and R. Schofield, 'Nominal record linkage by computer and the logic of family reconstitution', in E.A. Wrigley (ed.), *Identifying people in the past* (London, 1973), pp. 64-101.

3       K. Schürer, J. Oeppen and R Schofield, 'Theory and methodology: an example from historical demography', in P. Denley, S. Fogelvik and C. Harvey (eds), *History and Computing II* (Manchester, 1989), pp. 130-41.

4       As an example of the extent of standardisation involved, it might be noted that the 23,558 *Surname* strings recorded in the Database are reduced to 3,081 *Scode* strings.

5       Those which we held to be synonymous, such as Tailor/Taylor and Plaisterer/Plasterer share a common *Oclv4* string.

6       I. Winchester, 'A brief survey of the algorithmic, mathematical and philosophical literature relevant in historical record linkage' in Wrigley (ed.), *Identifying people in the past*, pp. 141-9.

7       The Guth algorithm is described in G. Guth, 'Surname spellings and computerised record linkage', *Historical Methods*, 10 (1976), pp. 10-19; the algorithm of the New York State Intelligence Information System is described in H.B. Newcombe, *Handbook of record linkage: methods for health and statistical studies, administration, and business* (Oxford, 1988), pp. 182-3.

[8]   Thrice ruined 'by his propensity for drinking and gaming' Simon
      Place experienced social, occupational and spatial mobility. In the
      early 1770s he worked as a bailiff for Marshalsea Court; he is found in
      **P1774** described as a gentleman living in the Strand. But a statute of
      1779 against frivolous and vexatious arrests removed much of his
      business, and he took the lease of *The King's Arms* in nearby Arundel
      Street. He is found at this address in **P1780** and **P1784**, latterly de-
      scribed as a victualler. See M. Thale (ed.), *The autobiography of
      Francis Place, 1771-1854* (Cambridge, 1972), pp. 22-33.

[9]   R.J. Morris, 'Data source to data base: the history of the British
      bourgeoisie and computer assisted research', in R. Metz, E. van Cau-
      wenberghe and R. van der Voort (eds), *Historical information systems
      Session B-12b*, Proceedings of the 10th international economic history
      congress, Leuven, August 1990 (Leuven, 1990), p. 60.

[10]  Winchester, 'On referring to ordinary historical persons' in Wrigley
      (ed.), *Identifying people in the past*, pp. 17-40.

[11]  It will be noted that a different measure of confidence is used here
      than the arbitrary weighting system  described in Harvey and Green,
      'Record linkage algorithms: efficiency, selection and relative confi-
      dence'. The confidence measure described here strikes us as better
      than that used by Harvey and Green, as it is derived from the data;
      moreover, the former work was explicitly descriptive of the methodol-
      ogy underlying Green, 'Thesis'.

[12]  Parochial political committees existed intermittently throughout the
      period, although few of their papers have survived. The papers of the
      committee in the parish of St Margaret and St John in the years 1818-
      20 (WAC E/3349) are an exception. The committee's chairman,
      Simon Stephenson, was well-placed to act in the parish of which he
      was the Vestry Clerk. Meanwhile the Vestries of St Margaret and St
      John regularly endorsed candidates, and provided rate collectors to
      attend at the hustings to check the rate book entries of voters. For
      parochial clubs, see T.W. Copeland (ed.), *The correspondence of
      Edmund Burke* (10 vols, Cambridge, 1958-78), v, p. 410, and D.E.
      Ginter (ed.), *Whig organization in the general election of 1790:
      selections from the Blair Adams papers* (Berkeley, Ca., 1967), p. 95.

[13]  See P. Jupp (ed), *British and Irish elections, 1784-1831* (Newton
      Abbot, 1973), pp. 127-8 for the use of the printed poll book of 1818 by
      Hobhouse's canvassers in 1819, and WAC E/3349/4/37 for the similar
      use of the poll book by their opponents.

[14]  This section draws heavily upon C. Harvey, E.M. Green and P.J.
      Corfield, 'Record linkage theory and practice: an experiment in the

application of multiple pass linkage algorithms', *History and Computing*, 8 (1996), pp. 78-89.

15     For example, the voting record of Simon Place, referred to above, would not be linked algorithmically before the thirty-seventh iteration or with the implementation of Algorithm 37.

# 7

# Overview

Among Herbert Butterfield's criticisms of Namier's prosopographical techniques was that the method treated people as automata responding to material pressures. 'Human beings are the carriers of ideas', he wrote, 'as well as the repositories of vested interests'.[1] And yet there is a danger of reading 'not' for Butterfield's more cautious 'as well as', and of throwing out the baby with the bath water. As they sail their uncharted seas, historians navigate a narrow channel between the Scylla of deterministic materialism and the Charybdis of post-modern fog.

To date, a number of publications have recorded the construction, interrogation and interpretation of the Westminster Historical Database. These fall into three main categories. The first and most extensive formulation of the authors' current research is contained in Edmund Green's London doctoral thesis.[2] There is also a short account of the Database in Harvey and Press.[3] A second category of material from the Database has been used to throw significant light on the problem of socio-economic classification. This is found in Green's demonstration of the diversity of financial interests accommodated within any one given occupational category.[4] A third set of short articles have been concerned with technical problems of record linkage using the Database for the purpose of experiment. These indicate the growing technical sophistication that modern computing makes available.[5]

These publications indicate what has been achieved so far; and what beckons for the future. Historically, there is much yet to be learned about the socio-economic patterns behind the complex voting history of Westminster. Did a Thompsonian class war lie either behind the Whig assaults upon the Pitt government in the 1780s? or behind the radical challenge to the wartime coalition in the 1790s and 1800s?[6] Can significant residential, rating or occupational groups be detected as consistent political forces in this period? Or was electoral motivation influenced by other factors, not incorporated in the Database (such as religious affiliation)? The authors intend to explore further the ramifications of electoral choice – to show both what can be known with confidence and what cannot. In addition, the occupational profile of Westminster will be analysed, as a contribution to the debates about the long-term development of the metropolitan economy at the point in time when London was emerging as the capital of a mighty world-wide trading empire.

The Westminster Historical Database lies on the cusp between historical social science and scientific history: as far as possible, it seeks precision in an imprecise past. The Database records systematically a mass of specific electoral data relating to a large and hotly contested constituency over a period of more than fifty years. It constitutes a flexible and powerful historical source that can be interrogated not only to test a number of technical questions relating to voter identification and voter choice in history, but simultaneously to throw light upon specific questions relating to the social context of Westminster's electoral politics. Moreover, it should serve in the future as a foundation stone for the comparative study of electoral behaviour, political allegiance and social structure within England and beyond.

This said, those responsible for the creation of the Westminster Historical Database are well aware of the limitations imposed upon it by the nature of the source material. Its greatest strength lies in the Poll Book tables, and within them in the data on voting behaviour. No other surviving data from the eighteenth century is so robust. And yet it is important to remember the limitations of such behavioural data. It remains exceedingly difficult to infer the motivation that lay behind the act of voting, and, if they are to develop convincing interpretations of problems, issues and events in the past, users will need sensitively to combine the 'hard' information yielded by the Database with the more qualitative evidence found elsewhere.

With this caveat, the authors are sure that the Westminster Historical Database will become a reference point for the many sub-disciplines of history and the social sciences. Demographers, family historians and genealogists have the opportunity, through record linkage, to explore the lives of individuals, families and communities over a long period of time. Economic, social and labour historians will find much to interest them in the copious data on occupations and the related data on property tax values. Political historians and political scientists will have before them a unique resource: individual level data recording tens of thousands of acts of voting in a tumultuous and immensely rich political setting. Geographers and urban historians equally may delight in the fact that the data relating to people, occupations, property values and voting become richer through the addition of a spatial dimension: we know not only how people claimed to earn a living and how they voted, but also where they lived and the quality of the property they inhabited.

It is clear also that value is added to information by linking it with other information. We recognise that the data offered here will become still richer by adding further sources to it. Within the Westminster context, a handful of key sources structured on a 'name and address' basis akin to that in the Database include, first, the rate books for all elections for which poll book data survive; secondly, the surviving printed poll books for the elections of 1837 and 1841, together with the annotated electoral register of 1851;[7] thirdly, the census of 1851; fourthly, the Sun Fire Insurance policies of the 1780s, available in machine-readable form; and finally, registers of the tax on male servants in 1780, also available in machine-readable form.

Beyond Westminster, there is clearly a pressing need to re-create the history of electoral behaviour in England for the period before 1872. Many thousands of poll books survive, and it has been shown that they constitute a rich source for exploration of the standing and behaviour of ordinary Englishmen over almost two centuries. It is to be hoped that the publication of the Westminster Historical Database will serve as both an inspiration and a model for others to do some of this work. An inspiration because there are hundreds of constituencies for which the surviving records are manageable in extent and well suited to the interests and aptitudes of local enthusiasts who can bring to the subject both committed hard work and specialist local knowledge. And a model because, if it is to be done, it is right that it should be done consistently and done well. Only by consistent and meticulous data entry can comparable data be gathered, and comparable results obtained.

Our intention in writing this short book has been to document the Westminster Historical Database to a standard beyond that which has hitherto prevailed and to indicate how scholars might make the most of the resource. We firmly believe that advances in historical interpretation and the quality of historical writing depend crucially upon access to true and reliable sources. We see the Westminster Historical Database as part of a new academic paradigm, of the publication of electronic editions of sources complete with critical apparatus, of collaborative research and of sharing resources. We hope that others will have as much pleasure in using the Database as we have had in its creation.

*Notes*

[1]    H. Butterfield, *George III and the historians* (1957), p. 211.

[2]    Green, 'Thesis'.

[3]    E.M. Green, 'Analysing social structure and political behaviour using poll and rate books: the Westminster Historical Database', in C. Harvey and J. Press, *Databases in historical research: theory, methods and applications* (1996), pp. 185-7.

[4]    E.M. Green, 'Taxonomy of occupations', in Corfield and Keene (eds), *Work in towns*, pp. 164-81.

[5]    E.M. Green, 'Social structure and political behaviour in Westminster, 1784-88', in P. Denley, S. Fogelvik and C. Harvey (eds), *History and computing II* (Manchester, 1989), pp. 239-42; Harvey and Green, 'Record linkage algorithms', pp. 143-52, and Harvey, Green and Corfield, 'Record linkage theory and practice', pp. 78-89.

[6]    E.P. Thompson, *The making of the English working class*, (1963; 2nd edn, Harmondsworth, 1968).

[7]    Anon., *A poll taken on Wednesday, 26 July, 1837, for the election of two members to represent the City of Westminster in parliament* (1837); Anon., *A poll taken on Wednesday, 30 June, 1841, for the election of two members to represent the City of Westminster in parliament* (1841); Anon., *A list of persons entitled to vote in the election of two members for the City and Liberty of Westminster* (1851). The annotated copy of this electoral register is held at the Institute of Historical Research, London.

# Select Bibliography

For ease of use this bibliography is divided into classified sections. Some items in the sections on record linkage, occupational classification and electoral behaviour are aimed at readers with prior knowledge of computer-based historical psephology. The section on English history is aimed rather more at the 'general reader': to those who last studied history at school, who remember that the late eighteenth century saw the Industrial Revolution, and whose views of electioneering derive from the Eatanswill election in *The Pickwick Papers*. The section on London history includes both specialist material and more general social history. Details of biographical studies of politicians who stood as candidates in Westminster are to be found in the notes to Chapter 3, above.

## 1 Historical computing

S. Anderson, 'The future of the present: the ESRC Data Archive as a resource centre of the future', *History and Computing*, 4 (1992), pp. 191-6.

P. Denley, 'Models, sources and users: historical database design in the 1990s', *History and Computing*, 6 (1994), pp. 33-43.

P. Denley and D. Hopkin (eds), *History and computing* (Manchester, 1987).

P. Denley, S. Fogelvik and C. Harvey (eds), *History and computing II* (Manchester, 1989).

C. Harvey and J. Press, *Databases in historical research: theory, methods and applications* (1996).

D.I. Greenstein, *A historian's guide to computing* (Oxford, 1994).

E. Mawdsley, N. Morgan, L. Richmond and R. Trainor (eds), *History and computing III* (Manchester, 1990).

E. Mawdsley and T. Munck, *Computing for historians: an introductory guide* (Manchester, 1993).

## 2 Record linkage

P. Adman, S.W. Baskerville and K.F. Beedham, 'Computer-assisted record linkage: or how best to optimise links without generating errors', *History and Computing*, 4 (1992), pp. 2-15.

J. Atack, F. Bateman and M.E. Gregson, '"Matchmaker, matchmaker, make me a match": a general personal computer-based matching program for historical research', *Historical Methods*, 25 (1992), pp. 53-65.

J.A. Baldwin, E.D. Acheson and W.J. Graham (eds), *Textbook of medical record linkage* (Oxford, 1987).

S.W. Baskerville, '"Preferred linkage" and the analysis of voter behaviour in eighteenth-century England', *History and Computing*, 1 (1989), pp. 112-20.

I.P. Felligi and A.B. Sunter, 'A theory for record linkage', *Journal of the American Statistical Association*, 64 (1969), pp. 1183-1210.

G. Guth, 'Surname spellings and computerized record linkage', *Historical Methods Newsletter*, 10 (1976), pp. 10-19.

C. Harvey and E.M. Green, 'Record linkage algorithms: efficiency, selection and relative confidence', *History and Computing*, 6 (1994), pp. 143-52.

C. Harvey, E.M. Green and P.J. Corfield, 'Record linkage theory and practice: an experiment in the application of multiple pass linkage algorithms', *History and Computing*, 8 (1996), pp. 78-89.

T. Hershberg, A. Burstein and R. Dockhorn, 'Record linkage', *Historical Methods Newsletter*, 9 (1975/6), pp. 137-63.

M.B. Katz, 'Record linkage for Everyman: a semi-automated process', *Historical Methods Newsletter*, 5 (1972), pp. 144-50.

B. Kilss and W. Alvery (eds), *Record linkage techniques - 1985* (Washington D.C., 1985).

B. Kilss and B. Jameson (eds), *Statistics of income and related administrative records research: 1988-9* (Washington D.C., 1990).

S. King, 'Record linkage in a protoindustrial community', *History and Computing*, 4 (1992), pp. 27-33.

G. Morton, 'Presenting the self: record linkage and referring to ordinary historical persons', *History and Computing*, 6 (1994), pp. 12-20.

H.B. Newcombe, *Handbook of record linkage: methods for health and statistical studies, administration, and business* (Oxford, 1988).

L. Nygaard, 'Name standardisation in record linking: an improved algorithmic strategy', *History and Computing*, 4 (1992), pp. 63-74.

J.A. Phillips, 'Achieving a critical mass while avoiding an explosion', *Journal of Interdisciplinary History*, 9 (1978), pp. 493-508.

S. Richardson, 'Letter-cluster sampling and nominal record linkage', *History and Computing*, 6 (1994), pp. 168-77.

I. Winchester, 'The linkage of historical records by man and computer: techniques and problems', *Journal of Interdisciplinary History*, 1 (1970), pp. 107-24.

I. Winchester, 'What every historian needs to know about record linkage for the microcomputer era', *Historical Methods*, 25 (1992), pp. 149-65.

E.A. Wrigley (ed.), *Identifying people in the past* (1973).

E.A. Wrigley, R.S. Davies, J.E. Oeppen and R.S. Schofield, *English population history from family reconstitution* (Cambridge, 1997).

## 3 Occupational classification

W.A. Armstrong, 'The use of information about occupation, part 1: a basis for social stratification; part 2: an industrial classification, 1841-91', in E.A. Wrigley (ed.), *Nineteenth-century society: essays in the use of quantitative methods for the study of social data* (Cambridge, 1972), pp. 191-310.

C. Booth, 'Occupations of the people of the United Kingdom, 1801-81', *Journal of the Royal Statistical Society* [of London], 49 (1886), pp. 314-444.

R. Campbell, *The London Tradesman* (1747; reprinted Newton Abbot, 1969).

P.J. Corfield, 'Class by name and number in eighteenth-century Britain', in idem (ed.), *Language, history and class* (Oxford, 1991), pp. 101-30.

P.J. Corfield, 'The Rivals: landed and other gentlemen', in N.B. Harte and R. Quinault (eds), *Land and society in Britain: es-*

*says for F.M.L. Thompson* (Manchester, 1996), pp. 1-33.

P.J. Corfield and D. Keene (eds), *Work in towns, 850-1850* (Leicester, 1990).

H. Diederiks and M. Balkestein (eds), *Occupational titles and their classification: the case of the textile trade in past times* (Göttingen: Max Planck Institut für Geschichte, 1995).

P. Glennie, *"Distinguishing men's trades": occupational sources and debates for pre-census England* (1990).

T. Hershberg and R. Dockhorn, 'Occupational classification', *Historical Methods Newsletter*, 9 (1975/6), pp. 59-98.

E. Higgs, 'The struggle for the occupational census, 1841-1911', in R.M. MacLeod (ed.), *Government and expertise: specialists, administrators and professionals, 1860-1919* (Cambridge, 1988), pp. 73-86.

E. Higgs, *Making sense of the census: the manuscript returns for England and Wales, 1801-1901* (1989).

E. Higgs, *A clearer sense of the census: the Victorian censuses and historical research* (1996).

M.B. Katz, 'Occupational classification in history', *Journal of Interdisciplinary History*, 3 (1972/3), pp. 63-88.

R. Lawton (ed.), *The census and the social structure: an interpretative guide to nineteenth-century censuses for England and Wales* (1978), esp. essays by Bellamy and Banks, pp. 165-223.

P. Lindert, 'English occupations, 1670-1811', *Journal of Economic History*, 40 (1980), pp. 685-712.

D. and J. Mills, 'Occupation and social stratification revisited: the census enumerators' books in Victorian Britain', *Urban History Yearbook 1989* (1989), pp. 63-77.

D. Mills and K. Schürer (eds), *Local communities in the Victorian census enumerators' books*, (Oxford, 1996).

R.J. Morris, 'Occupational coding: principles and examples', *Historical Social Research*, 15 (1990), pp. 3-29.

J. Patten, 'Urban occupations in pre-industrial England', *Transactions of the Institute of British Geographers*, new series, 2 (1977), pp. 296-313.

G. Routh, *Occupations of the people of Great Britain, 1801-1981: with a compendium of a paper ... by Charles Booth* (1987).

K. Schürer and H. Diederiks (eds), *The use of occupations in historical analysis* (Göttingen: Max Planck Institut für Geschichte, 1993).

S.R.S. Szreter, 'The genesis of the Registrar General's social classification of occupations', *British Journal of Sociology*, 35
(1984), pp. 522-46.

D.J. Treiman, *Occupational prestige in comparative perspective*
(New York, 1977).


## 4 Political, economic and social history of England, c. 1750-1820

J. Brewer, *Party ideology and popular politics at the accession of
George III* (Cambridge, 1976).

J.Brewer, 'Commercialization and politics', in N. McKendrick, J.
Brewer and J.H. Plumb, *The birth of a consumer society: the
commercialization of eighteenth-century England* (1982), pp.
197-262.

J. Brewer (ed.), *The common people and politics, 1750-1790s*
(Cambridge, 1986).

J. Brewer, *The pleasures of the imagination: English culture in the
eighteenth century* (1997).

I.R. Christie, *Wars and revolutions: Britain, 1760-1815* (1982).

I.R. Christie, *Stress and stability in late eighteenth century Britain:
reflections on the British avoidance of revolution* (Oxford,
1984).

J.C.D. Clark, *English society, 1688-1832: ideology, social structure and political practice during the ancien regime*
(Cambridge, 1985).

M.J. Daunton, *Progress and poverty: an economic and social
history of Britain, 1700-1850* (Oxford, 1995).

H.T. Dickinson (ed.), *Caricatures and the constitution, 1760-1832*
(Cambridge, 1986).

H.T. Dickinson (ed.), *Britain and the French Revolution, 1789-
1815* (1989).

H.T. Dickinson, *The politics of the people in eighteenth-century
Britain* (1995).

D. Donald, *The age of caricature: satirical prints in the reign of
George III* (New Haven, Ct, 1996).

R.R. Dozier, *For King, constitution and country: the English
loyalists and the French Revolution* (Lexington, Ky, 1983).

J.A. Epstein, *Radical expression: political language, ritual and symbol in England, 1790-1850* (New York, 1994).

E.J. Evans, *The forging of the modern state: early industrial Britain, 1783-1870* (1983).

R. Floud and D. McCloskey (eds), *The economic history of Britain since 1700, vol. 1, 1700-1850* (Cambridge, 1981; 2$^{nd}$ edn, 1994).

D.E. Ginter (ed.), *Voting records of the British House of Commons, 1761-1820* (6 vols, 1995).

A. Goodwin, *The friends of liberty: the English democratic movement in the age of the French Revolution* (1979).

D. Hay and N. Rogers, *Eighteenth-century English society: shuttles and swords* (Oxford, 1997).

B.W. Hill, *British parliamentary parties, 1742-1832* (1985).

G. Holmes and D. Szechi, *The age of oligarchy: pre-industrial Britain, 1722-83* (1993).

P. Langford, *A polite and commercial people: England, 1727-83* (Oxford, 1989).

L.B. Namier, *The structure of politics at the accession of George III* (1929; 2$^{nd}$ ed., 1957).

L.B. Namier and J. Brooke (eds), *The House of Commons, 1754-90* (3 vols, 1964).

M. Philp (ed.), *The French revolution and British popular politics* (Cambridge, 1991).

F. O'Gorman, *The emergence of the British two-party system, 1760-1832* (1982).

R. Porter, *English society in the eighteenth century* (Harmondsworth, 1982).

N. Rogers, *Whigs and cities: popular politics in the age of Walpole and Pitt* (Oxford, 1989).

J. Rule, *Albion's people: English society, 1714-1815* (1992).

J. Rule, *The vital century: England's developing economy, 1714-1815* (1992).

R. Sedgwick (ed.), *The House of Commons, 1715-54* (2 vols, 1970).

E.P. Thompson, *The making of the English working class* (1963; 2$^{nd}$ ed., Harmondsworth, 1968).

E.P. Thompson, *Customs in common* (1991).

R.G. Thorne (ed.), *The House of Commons, 1790-1820* (5 vols, 1986).

D. Wahrman, *Imagining the middle class: the political representa-*

*tion of class in Britain, c. 1780-1840* (Cambridge, 1995).

D. Worrall, *Radical culture: discourse, resistance and surveillance, 1790-1820* (1992).

K. Wilson, *The sense of the people: politics, culture and imperialism in England, 1715-85* (Cambridge, 1995).


## 5  Electoral behaviour in Britain

J.E. Bradley, *Religion, revolution, and English radicalism: nonconformity in eighteenth-century politics and society* (Cambridge, 1990).

J. Cannon, 'Poll books', *History*, 47 (1962), pp. 166-9.

M. Clayton, 'Voter choice in a patronage borough: Haslemere, 1754-80', *Parliamentary History*, 15 (1996), pp. 151-72.

R.W. Davis, *Political change and continuity, 1760-1885: a Buckinghamshire study* (Newton Abbot, 1972).

M. Drake, 'The mid-Victorian voter', *Journal of Interdisciplinary History*, 1 (1971), pp. 473-90.

M. Drake (ed.), *Introduction to historical psephology* (Milton Keynes, 1982).

D. Fraser, *Urban politics in Victorian England: the structure of politics in Victorian cities* (Leicester, 1976).

P. Jupp (ed.), *British and Irish elections, 1784-1831* (Newton Abbot, 1973).

N. Landau, 'Independence, deference, and voter participation: the behaviour of the electorate in early eighteenth-century Kent', *Historical Journal*, 22 (1979), pp. 561-83.

J. Lawrence and M. Taylor (eds), *Party, state and society: electoral behaviour in Britain since 1820* (Aldershot, 1996).

J.C. Mitchell, 'Electoral strategy under open voting', *Public Choice*, 28 (1976), pp. 17-35.

J.C. Mitchell and J. Cornford, 'The political demography of Cambridge, 1832-68', *Albion*, 9 (1977), pp. 242-72.

D.C. Moore, 'The other face of reform', *Victorian Studies*, 4 (1961), pp. 7-34.

D.C. Moore, *The politics of deference: a study of the mid-nineteenth century English political system* (Hassocks, 1976).

R.J. Morris, *Class, sect and party: the making of the British middle class, Leeds, 1820-50* (Manchester, 1990).

R.S. Neale, *Class and ideology in the nineteenth century* (1972).

T.J. Nossiter, *Influence, opinion and political idioms in reformed England: case studies from the north east, 1832-74* (Hassocks, 1975).

F. O'Gorman, 'Electoral deference in unreformed England, 1760-1832', *Journal of Modern History*, 56 (1984), pp. 391-429.

F. O'Gorman, *Voters, patrons and parties: the unreformed electoral system of Hanoverian England, 1734-1832* (Oxford, 1989).

F. O'Gorman, 'Campaign rituals and ceremonies: the social meaning of elections in England, 1780-1860', *Past and Present*, 135 (1992), pp. 79-115.

J.A. Phillips, *Electoral behavior in unreformed England: plumpers, splitters and straights* (Princeton, 1982).

J.A. Phillips, *The Great Reform Bill in the boroughs: English electoral behaviour, 1818-41* (Oxford, 1992).

J.A. Phillips (ed.), *Computing parliamentary history: George III to Victoria* (Edinburgh, 1994).

J.A. Phillips and C. Wetherell, 'Event history analysis and electoral behaviour: a case study, Northampton, 1818-41', in J. Smets (ed.), *Histoire et informatique* (Montpellier, 1992), pp. 537-53.

J.A. Phillips and C. Wetherell, 'Probability and political behaviour: a case study of the Municipal Corporations Act of 1835', *History and Computing*, 5 (1993), pp. 135-53.

J.A. Phillips and C. Wetherell, 'The Great Reform Act of 1832 and the political modernization of England', *American Historical Review*, 100 (1995), pp. 411-36.

J. Sims (ed.), *Handlist of British parliamentary poll books* (Leicester, 1984).

W.A. Speck and W.A. Gray, 'Computer analysis of poll books: an initial report', *Bulletin of the Institute of Historical Research*, 43 (1970), pp. 105-12.

W.A. Speck and W.A. Gray, 'Londoners at the polls under Anne and George I', *Guildhall Studies in London History*, 1 (1975), pp. 253-62.

W.A. Speck, W.A. Gray and R. Hopkinson, 'Computer analysis of poll books: a further report', *Bulletin of the Institute of Historical Research*, 48 (1975), pp. 64-90.

J.R. Vincent, *Pollbooks: how Victorians voted* (Cambridge, 1967).

## 6 History of London and Westminster

Anon., *History of the Westminster election, containing every material occurrence, from its commencement on 1 April, to the final close of the poll, on 17 May* (1784; 2nd ed., 1785).

Anon., *History of the Westminster and Middlesex elections, in the month of November, 1806* (1807).

Anon., *An exposition of the circumstances which gave rise to the election of Sir Francis Burdett, Bt, for the City of Westminster* (1807).

Anon., *An authentic narrative of the events of the Westminster election* (1819).

M. Baer, *Theatre and disorder in late Georgian London* (Oxford, 1992).

H. Creaton (ed.), *Bibliography of printed works of London history to 1939* (1994).

D. Cruickshank and N. Burton, *Life in the Georgian city* (1990).

G.S. De Krey, *A fractured society: the politics of London in the first age of party, 1688-1715* (Oxford, 1985).

P. Earle, *The making of the English middle class: business, society and family life in London, 1660-1730* (1989).

P. Earle, *A city full of people: men and women of London, 1650-1750* (1994).

C. Fox (ed.), *London: world city, 1800-40* (New Haven, 1992).

M.D. George, *London life in the eighteenth century* (1925; 2nd edn, Harmondsworth, 1966).

D.R. Green, *From artisans to paupers: economic change and poverty in London, 1790-1870* (Aldershot, 1995).

E.M. Green, 'The taxonomy of occupations in late eighteenth-century Westminster', in P.J. Corfield and D. Keene (eds), *Work in towns, 850-1850* (Leicester, 1990), pp. 164-81.

J.A. Hone, *For the cause of truth: radicalism in London, 1796-1821* (Oxford, 1982).

R. Hyde (ed.), *The A to Z of Georgian London* (Lympne, 1982).

J. Landers, *Death and the metropolis: studies in the demographic history of London, 1670-1830* (Cambridge, 1993).

P. Laxton (ed.), *The A to Z of Regency London* (Lympne, 1985).

J.M. Main, 'Radical Westminster, 1807-20', *Historical Studies (Australia and New Zealand)*, 12 (1965-7), pp. 186-204.

D.R. McAdams, 'Electioneering techniques in populous constituencies, 1784-96', *Studies in Burke and his Time*, 14 (1972), pp. 23-53.

I. McCalman, *Radical underworld: prophets, revolutionaries and pornographers in London, 1795-1840* (Cambridge, 1988).

R. Porter, *London: a social history* (1994).

F. Pottle (ed.), *Boswell's London journal, 1762-3* (1950).

I. Prothero, *Artisans and politics in early nineteenth-century London: John Gast and his times* (Folkestone, 1979).

N. Rogers, 'Aristocratic clientage, trade and independency: popular politics in pre-radical Westminster', *Past and Present*, 61 (1973), pp. 70-106.

G. Rudé, 'The Middlesex electors of 1768-9', *English Historical Review*, 75 (1960), pp. 601-17.

G. Rudé, *Wilkes and liberty: a social study of 1763-74* (Oxford, 1962).

G. Rudé, *Paris and London in the eighteenth century: studies in popular protest* (1970).

G. Rudé, *Hanoverian London, 1714-1808* (1971).

J. Sainsbury, *Disaffected patriots: London supporters of revolutionary America, 1760-85* (Gloucester, 1987).

L.D. Schwarz, 'Income distribution and social structure in London in the late eighteenth century', *Economic History Review*, 2nd ser., 32 (1979), pp. 250-9.

L.D. Schwarz, 'Social class and social geography: the middle classes in London at the end of the eighteenth century', *Social History*, 7 (1982), pp. 167-85.

L.D. Schwarz, *London in the age of industrialisation: entrepreneurs, labour force and living conditions, 1700-1850* (Cambridge, 1992).

F.H.W. Sheppard, *London, 1808-70: the infernal wen* (1971).

P. Spence, *The birth of romantic radicalism: war, popular politics and English radical reformism, 1800-15* (Aldershot, 1996).

J. Stevenson (ed.), *London in the age of reform* (Oxford, 1977).

J. Summerson, *Georgian London* (1945; new edn, 1991).

L.S. Sutherland, *The City of London and the opposition to government, 1768-74: a study in the rise of metropolitan radicalism* (1959).

M. Thale (ed.), *The autobiography of Francis Place, 1771-1854* (Cambridge, 1972).

M. Thale (ed.), *Selections from the papers of the London Corre-sponding Society, 1792-9* (Cambridge, 1983).

W.E.S. Thomas, 'Radical Westminster' in idem., *The philosophic radicals: nine studies in theory and practice, 1817-41* (Oxford, 1979), pp. 46-94.

# Index

Throughout the index, the abbreviation WHD means Westminster Historical Database. Headwords in italics indicate fields; those in capitals indicate computer commands and functions. Page references in italics indicate tables, figures and plates; those in bold indicate maps.